ATTITUDE
IS
EVERYTHING
FOR
SUCCESS

Also by Keith D. Harrell

An Attitude of Gratitude: 21 Life Lessons

Attitude Is Everything: *10 Life-Changing Steps to Turning Attitude into Action*

Attitude Is Everything Cards

The Attitude Is Everything Workbook: *Strategies and Tools for Developing Personal and Professional Success*

The Attitude of Leadership: *Taking the Lead and Keeping It*

Please visit Hay House USA: **www.hayhouse.com**
Hay House Australia: **www.hayhouse.com.au**
Hay House UK: **www.hayhouse.co.uk**
Hay House South Africa: **orders@psdprom.co.za**

*Available through Hay House

ATTITUDE
IS
EVERYTHING
FOR
SUCCESS

SAY IT,
BELIEVE IT,
RECEIVE IT

Keith D. Harrell

HAY
HOUSE

HAY HOUSE, INC.
Carlsbad, California
London • Sydney • Johannesburg
Vancouver • Hong Kong

Published and distributed in the United States by: Hay House, Inc., P.O. Box 5100, Carlsbad, CA 92018-5100 • *Phone:* (760) 431-7695 or (800) 654-5126 • *Fax:* (760) 431-6948 or (800) 650-5115 • www.hayhouse.com • *Published and distributed in Australia by:* Hay House Australia, Ltd., 18/36 Ralph St., Alexandria NSW 2015 • *Phone:* 612-9669-4299 • *Fax:* 612-9669-4144 • www.hayhouse.com.au • *Published and distributed in the United Kingdom by:* Hay House UK, Ltd. • Unit 202, Canalot Studios • 222 Kensal Rd., London W10 5BN • *Phone:* 44-20-8962-1230 • *Fax:* 44-20-8962-1239 • www.hayhouse.co.uk • *Published and distributed in the Republic of South Africa by:* Hay House SA (Pty), Ltd., P.O. Box 990, Witkoppen 2068 • *Phone/Fax:* 2711-7012233 • orders@psdprom.co.za • *Distributed in Canada by:* Raincoast • 9050 Shaughnessy St., Vancouver, B.C. V6P 6E5 • *Phone:* (604) 323-7100 • *Fax:* (604) 323-2600

Editorial supervision: Jill Kramer   *Design:* Amy Rose Szalkiewicz

Library of Congress Cataloging-in-Publication Data

Harrell, Keith D.
   Attitude is everything for success : say it, believe it, receive it / Keith D. Harrell.
       p. cm.
   ISBN 1-4019-0201-4
   1. Attitude (Psychology) I. Title.
   BF327.H373 2004
   153.8'5—dc21

                                   2003012609

ISBN 1-4019-0201-4

07 06 05 04   4 3 2 1
1st printing, January 2004

Printed in the United States of America

This book is dedicated with the greatest love and affection to my family and friends for their love, support, and encouragement. And most important, to God for giving me everything— life, knowledge, wisdom, and the ability to do His work.

CONTENTS

INTRODUCTION

This book will clearly show you how having the right attitude is one of the master keys for successful living. You see, your attitude affects all of your interactions as well as the outcome of everything you do—so a positive attitude will help you navigate successfully through life, while a negative one will cement you into destructive patterns that doom you to failure.

The words you say fuel your attitude, so you must intentionally select helpful language in order to create the right conditions to attract success. If, after you make a mistake, you tell yourself, "I never do anything right," chances are good that you'll fail in your next attempt as well. However, if you see that you've made an error and instead say, "I make good decisions, and I learn something new from each one," you'll grow stronger through your life experiences. We all make mistakes now and then—if we didn't, we wouldn't be doing anything at all—but our attitude toward those mistakes is what determines whether or not they become setbacks or opportunities to grow.

When you realize the impact that certain words have over your life, you can choose powerful language rather than depleting, defeating terminology. And when you speak those empowering words, you'll gradually start to create the quality of life you desire. Yes, words alone are the guide to success.

During the past two decades, I've traveled around the country delivering keynote speeches to a wide variety of organizations, and in the process, I've had the privilege to talk to thousands of successful individuals from many walks of life. I noticed that all of them, without exception, repeatedly used words that they associated with their success and winning attitudes. I took notes and discovered 30 key terms these high-profile people used again and again. My feeling is that an empowering word for each day of the month will help give you the attitude "tune-up" needed for success. In this small volume, I've compiled those 30 key words—along with definitions, affirmations, personal anecdotes, insights, and daily quotes to motivate you to put these potent ideas into action.

In these rapidly changing, technology-driven times, many of us can't find the time to sit for a few minutes to be quiet, tap in to our inner spirits, relax, and unwind. With your hectic schedule, you may find it difficult to read even one chapter of the latest bestselling book on self-improvement or listen to your favorite motivational tape in an effort to refocus and find balance. Yet, ironically enough, such daunting daily demands make you need a word of inspiration or encouragement or a useful quote even more—*anything* to redirect your thinking, lift your spirits, center you, and get you back on course.

So, this book was written with your tight schedule in mind. Instead of trying to feed you a seven-course meal when you only have time for a small snack, I will give you juicy morsels of wisdom, a bite at a time, so you can learn tools to counteract your doubt-producing inner dialogue. Each morsel delivers knowledge and energy to help you navigate through challenging times.

When you find that you're in a hurry, yet you need that word, quote, or something to boost your attitude or self-esteem, pick up this book. Your answer, your motivation, your inspiration—your word tools—are within these pages. All the stories presented here are true, although some of the names have been changed to protect the privacy of the people involved. And after you read this book, you can add in your *own* true story of success!

Remember that *attitude is everything*—and the key to success is to *say it, believe it, and receive it.*

HOW TO USE THIS BOOK

This book is structured in a user-friendly, easy-to-read format. If you wish, you can start with Day 1, or you may prefer to pick the word best suited to the challenge you're facing on that particular day. You could also let the book fall open to a page, allowing circumstance or destiny guide you, or you might want to read a little bit at a time in sequence—whatever works best for you *is* best for you.

No matter where you start, as long as you read and reread the page of insights out loud, you *will* reprogram your attitude. Choose a word or a chapter, review the related section called "Say It, Believe It, Receive It" (each part of this section is explained in further detail below), and you're on your way to acquiring the attitudes that contribute to a more successful life!

Say It

You may not be aware of this, but the statements you use define you because they express your underlying beliefs. It's vitally important that you understand the power of the words you use with others and yourself. Your words define your reality, and you ultimately act on what you believe. While positive statements elevate and enrich you, negative statements deflate, undermine, and injure you. They hold you back from achieving what you desire by actually stealing your power. Words chosen and spoken wisely transform, empower, inspire, nurture, and heal—while carelessly chosen words undercut success, sabotage progress, and limit your reality.

Think about something in your life that you thought you wanted to do or achieve but never did. For example, I know a woman named Barbara who told me that when she was young, she wanted to become a veterinarian. She loved animals and felt sure that she knew her calling from a very young age. However, she had difficulty understanding mathematical concepts, and she soon fell behind. As a result of losing out on the basics of math in grammar school, she found the subject a mystery at every level, and she barely squeezed by in algebra and other forms of mathematics in high school and college. Since Barbara knew that she needed high math scores to get into veterinary school, she never even took the required prerequisites—instead, she went on to major in journalism, where math wasn't a big issue. Why did she miss out on becoming a veterinarian? Because she told herself she wasn't good enough in math. She heard the little voice in her head saying, "You'll never get into veterinary school with your low math skills, so you'd better find some other way to make a living."

Was the culprit really her poor math skills, or was it her self-talk? You guessed it—it was the latter. If Barbara had simply changed her inner dialogue to a statement such as "I can learn anything I set my mind to," she would have found the tutors and books necessary to help her raise her skills to the required level. Instead, she said, "I'll never be good in math" . . . and she wasn't. Fortunately, she found a calling elsewhere, but a deep lesson lurks in the fact that she listened to her negative voice instead of replacing it with a positive one.

Now, let's go back to the thing you wanted when you were younger, but never achieved. What types of negative self-talk kept you from your goal? If you had it to do over, how would you change that self-talk so that you could achieve your desire?

I've got some good news for you—it's never too late to start! A great place to begin is with positive affirmations, which I've assembled into three parts in this book: *I acknowledge . . . I possess . . .* and *I am.* You see, "I statements" such as these put the responsibility for your feelings, actions, and successes right where they belong: on you. Each "I statement," when said with belief and authority, positively affects your attitude, focuses your thinking, and leads you to a course of productive action that will help you become the person you want to be and have the things you want to have.

Repeat these affirmations several times a day, *every* day, to reprogram your subconscious and set firmly in your mind each divine statement of truth. At the moment you first say these words, you may not feel or believe what you say, but follow the advice in Romans 4:17 and ". . . speak those things that be not as if they were." Think about the first time you rode a bike, skated, drove a stick-shift car, or used a computer: At first you probably felt awkward, uncomfortable, unnatural, and even a little fearful—yet with practice, you acquired the skills you needed to overcome your initial awkwardness. Soon you performed well, easily, effectively, and almost automatically. By the same token, positive affirmations for success may also feel awkward at first, but just like learning to ride that bicycle, once you've repeated the right words and quotes out loud long enough, you'll feel comfortable with the procedure.

Continue to repeat the statements for the next 30 days, and watch the change in your thinking and your attitude. Ultimately, you'll experience success in whichever way you've defined it.

Believe It

In this section, I'll explain how the right words can empower you. As you think of each of the words in this book, I'd like you to remember a positive incident in your life and recall your attitude, your mind-set, and your feelings. Then, as you read the "Believe It" section, focus on how each word recharges and renews your attitude and enhances your success.

For example, the particular word might elicit memories of something as small as when your grade-school teacher held up your paper and told the class it was a good example of neatness. Perhaps your college roommate complimented you on your choice of clothes. Maybe you entered a contest and won, or made the winning run in a ball game. Reach into your memories and pull out a positive experience like that—think about the words others used and how they made you feel, and remember your emotions, the overwhelming sense of joy you experienced at the time. This exercise helps you remember that great things have happened to you . . . and if you believe they can happen again, they will.

I'll also give you real-life examples of success stories in everyday situations—that is, you'll see how others have benefited from practicing the principle of belief. As you read their stories, think of an incident in your own life when you role-modeled (or didn't) the quality of belief. Reflect on whether you "own" this attitude or whether you need to increase your determination to acquire it.

Receive It

In this stage, you'll internalize and visualize the "attitude" words you've been saying. You'll walk, talk, and act as if you own the characteristics you seek and have already received the things you want. In other words, you'll "fake it till you make it." When you act "as if" you've already achieved and received what you want, you expedite the attitude-acquisition process, because you're *doing* it, not merely *thinking* it. You'll move into the action that will bring you closer to having what you truly desire.

Let's say, for instance, that you want to be promoted to manager of your department. If you act as if you already *are* the manager, you'll dress the part, arrive early to work, tackle aggressive projects that prove your worth to the company, and make yourself visible. Soon you'll see the rewards in a promotion or something even better.

Now, if you have a presentation to give, you can talk yourself into feeling and acting more self-assured by saying the **Day 11—*Confidence*** affirmations out loud, and turn panic into poise. And if you feel aimless, you can make your life more meaningful by studying **Day 24—*Purpose,*** and clarify why you're here and what you want to accomplish.

As you discover the power of the 30 key words I'm about to give you, you'll begin to spot other terms that empower and inspire you as well. Add them to your personal list and incorporate them into your vocabulary. Follow the format I've shared in this book, and you'll constantly and consciously choose language that continues to support your success.

Daily Quotes

We all have favorite quotes and sayings . . . why do we love them so much? Perhaps because quotes are succinct, eloquent statements that often capture the essence of a divine truth better than we can express in our own words. Quotes can be funny, profound, thought-provoking, and timeless, and they often use the smallest number of words to deliver a strong message or an enlightening insight.

Review the quotes in this book and select the ones that resonate with you—then repeat them until you can say them from memory. When you find yourself faced with a challenge, recite the appropriate quote again and again to keep your thoughts *con*structive instead of *de*structive. Reprogram your attitude with the enduring and wise observations from some of the greatest philosophers and humorists on Earth. And if you're in a rut, grab one of these quotes and affirmations to reprogram your attitude. Remember, *the right words each day help keep failure away.*

Let's get working on that attitude!

achievement To accomplish
or attain by work or effort.

ACh
IeVe
meNT

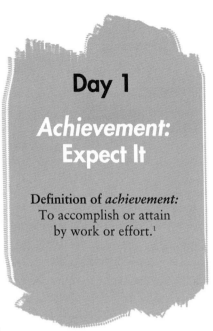

Day 1

Achievement: Expect It

Definition of *achievement:*
To accomplish or attain
by work or effort.[1]

Say It

As you speak the following phrases, believe and embrace them. Visualize yourself having what you state—possess it. Notice how your voice and body respond to each "I" statement:

- *I acknowledge achievement in all areas of my life.*

- *I possess the skills and talents to achieve anything.*

[1] All definitions are from *Webster's II New Riverside Dictionary, Revised Edition.*

- *I am an achiever.*

- *I am realizing the positive outcomes I truly desire.*

- *I am thankful for all of my achievements, no matter how small.*

Believe It

You can go beyond your current situation—in fact, more than you ever imagined is within your reach, because it's within *you.* All it takes is the right attitude. To maintain that attitude, celebrate every victory. Make each one special, because small victories are living proof that you can accomplish things, and they lead to even greater triumphs.

Recently I've had several major achievements, including getting an article published in *The Wall Street Journal* and having my books published by prominent companies. While these achievements are important, they're no more significant than completing a chore, putting my neighbor's paper on his porch to get it out of the rain, calling my mom to tell her I love her, resisting temptation, or leading an honest life.

Reread the definition of *achievement* again. Notice that it contains the words *work* and *effort*. Thanks to a great coach, I learned early in life that achieving what I want often has more to do with effort than talent. When I was nine years old, Sarge, my coach, selected me for an all-star baseball team, much to my surprise. I was tall and gangly and didn't think I was a good enough player to make the team. Sarge explained why he picked me: "A player can have great skills, but his talent won't mean much if he doesn't apply himself and get the job done. I'd rather have someone on my team who works hard, because I know he's always going to be getting better."

As I look back on my life now, I attribute much of my professional success to my continued willingness to hustle and do whatever is necessary to get the job done. Procrastination never became an issue for me because I've been clear that I can get what I want simply by working at it. Today, anytime I have difficulty with something, whether it's lowering my golf handicap or memorizing a new keynote speech, I remind myself that I can achieve it when I'm ready to invest the time and effort needed to complete the task. Thanks, Sarge, for teaching me such a valuable lesson.

Receive It

Think of something you want to achieve: Would you like to go back to school? Run a marathon? Master a new language? Learn to paint? Landscape your yard? Become an independent consultant? Write a book? Let your imagination take you to whatever heights it wants to go.

Now envision what's keeping you from reaching your goal. Chances are good that the barriers aren't on the outside—they're within you. Are you procrastinating, even on seemingly important projects? Are you afraid that you don't have the talent to accomplish your goal? Do you think you don't have the time? Do you see failure before you even begin?

If you answered yes to any of these questions, think again. You can turn procrastination into hustle and start working toward your objective. Mentally fast-forward to that time when you will have achieved your goal. Bask in the glow of success. Enjoy the feeling of attaining your desire. Feel it. Sense it. Picture it in your mind. Now believe it. Receive the sensation of accomplishment, and you'll be inspired to achieve even greater things.

Today, decide what you need to do to overcome any barriers to your achievement, put a plan together, and take the first step.

ᩤ

Daily Quotes

"Achievement is not a thing to be waited for, it is a thing to go after."

— Anonymous

"We have got but one life here. It pays, no matter what comes after it, to try and do things, to accomplish things in this life and not merely to have a soft and pleasant time."

— Theodore Roosevelt

"Achievement starts when you know that your present place in life does not determine how far you will go. Its only purpose is to remind you where you started."

— Keith D. Harrell

ᩤ ᩤ ᩤ

A manner, process,
or method of performing
action an act or deed; habitual or vigorous
activity or energy; movement;
motion; a force that causes change.

AcTI
ON

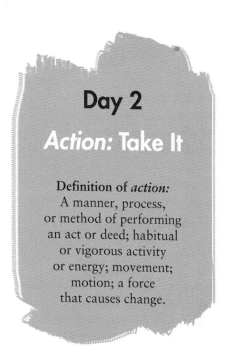

Day 2

Action: Take It

Definition of *action:*
A manner, process,
or method of performing
an act or deed; habitual
or vigorous activity
or energy; movement;
motion; a force
that causes change.

Say It

As you speak the following phrases, believe and embrace them. Visualize yourself having what you state—possess it. Notice how your voice and body respond to each "I" statement:

- *I acknowledge the things I need to take action on in my life.*

- *I possess the attitude and skills needed to take action.*

- *I am proactive.*

- *I am consciously acting upon my thoughts and producing the desired outcomes.*

- *I am winning in life by turning my attitude into action.*

Believe It

Not many of us can recall all the laws of physics, but most of us remember these: A body in motion tends to stay in motion, and a body at rest tends to stay at rest. So a stationary body continues to have no action, but a moving body keeps going . . . could life really be that simple?

Yes, it can. Life can be put as simply as this: Do nothing, and nothing gets done; do something, and many things get set into motion. We can't sit around expecting success to come to us—we have to break out of our inertia and take action to get what we want.

One of the best contemporary practitioners of the concept of "taking action" is a man named Nido Qubein. Nido left the Middle East and came to America as a teenager with just $50 in his pocket. Today he is the president and CEO of the Great Harvest Bread Company, owner of several other businesses, and a member of the board of directors for numerous charitable organizations. How did Nido accomplish so much? Well, for one thing, he didn't sit down and bemoan the challenging circumstances life had given him, nor did he wait for people to rescue him. He was *proactive*, rather than *reactive*. He took action and set himself in motion, and he hasn't stopped since. Nido is the first to admit that everything he holds dear is a result of acting on his own behalf because he simply wasn't willing to remain in those unfavorable conditions.

Regardless of what you're doing in life, you need to take action. For example, when I'm on the road, I check my voice mail often because I want to take action and get back to people as quickly as possible. I'm convinced that this habit has benefited my business, for this seemingly small gesture shows clients, family members, and friends how important they are to me.

What are you doing to put action into your plan? What first step can you take to set you on the path to your goal? Do you need to take a course, read a book, make a phone call, create a proposal, or write a letter? Take that step today, and put your plan into action.

Receive It

Are there less-than-ideal circumstances in your life? What's happening that you don't like? What do you want that you don't have yet? Ask, and you shall receive; seek, and you shall find. You've got to know what you want, because whatever you're seeking will then start to seek you. Knock, and the door will be opened. Don't wait to be rescued, and don't spend your energy complaining or worrying. Instead, define one thing you can do *today* that will take you one step closer to your ideal situation, your perfect life, or whatever goal or object you desire. Movement produces momentum. One step is all it takes to begin your journey, and as you continue to take steps, you'll move forward and leave the past behind. Also, be sure to celebrate each step you take, and enjoy the fact that you're on your path.

Daily Quotes

*"Action may not always bring happiness,
but there is no happiness without action."*

— Benjamin Disraeli

*"Action springs not from thought,
but from a readiness for responsibility."*

— Dietrich Bonhoeffer

*"Action will remove
the doubt that theory cannot solve."*

— Tehyi Hsieh

attitude

A state of feeling or mind about a particular person or situation; a position of the body or manner of carrying oneself: posture.

ATTi tUDE

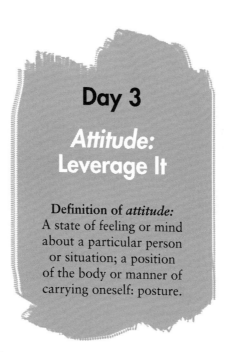

Day 3

Attitude:
Leverage It

Definition of *attitude*:
A state of feeling or mind
about a particular person
or situation; a position
of the body or manner of
carrying oneself: posture.

Say It

As you speak the following phrases, believe and
embrace them. Visualize yourself having what you
state—possess it. Notice how your voice and body
respond to each "I" statement:

- *I acknowledge the importance of maintaining a positive attitude in my life.*

- *I possess a positive attitude.*

- *I am positive.*

- *I am optimistic that good things will happen in my life.*

- *I am positive about what this day will bring. I rejoice and feel glad.*

Believe It

Attitude is a feeling, a mood, a mindset, an outlook, and most important, it defines your life.

You might not be able to choose your initial circumstances, but you can choose your attitude *toward* your circumstances. If you don't like your life, instead of wallowing in self-pity, see yourself changing it—sure enough, what you envision will come about. If want to be out of debt and you believe that you can do it, you will. If you wish you had a better job and believe that you're worthy of one, then before you know it, you'll take the steps to bring it about.

Here's how I make sure I start each day with a happy, self-assured attitude: The moment I wake up, I applaud the day—I actually clap in bed! Then I pray, thanking God for another day. My goal is to wake up with peace and joy in my spirit, and I find that when I start out with a great attitude, it's easy to maintain one throughout the day.

Receive It

Give yourself an attitude tune-up: What were your first thoughts when you woke up this morning? You had a vast range of choices, from "Woe is me; I have to drag myself out of bed and get to work" to "Hooray! It's a brand-new day in which I can do many wonderful things." So, were your thoughts positive or negative? If your thoughts were pessimistic, did you immediately replace them with optimistic ones? If they were positive, congratulate yourself and keep up the good work.

When you arrived at your place of work, how did you react to your fellow employees? Did you greet them with smiles when they asked how you were? Did you tell them that attitude is everything? Or did you just tell them, "I'm here—that's good enough"?

In case you think that having a strong belief that all will be fine is a brand-new philosophy, in the early 1900s French psychotherapist Émile Coué published a book called *Self Mastery Through Conscious Autosuggestion.* In it he suggests that every person, several times a day, should repeat this affirmation:

"Day by day in every way, I am getting better and better." Try it—first thing every morning, tell yourself that you're getting better every day. And believe it, because just by reading this book, you've set a process in motion that will bring to you what you want. You *are* getting better. It's already happening. You're in the process of receiving what you want.

Remember that your attitude determines your feelings, your feelings determine your actions, and your actions determine your results.

Daily Quotes

*"Life is 10 percent what you make it
and 90 percent how you take it."*

— Irving Berlin

*"Attitude—it's the control center for your life;
it will determine how high you will go
or how low you will stay."*

— Dr. Creflo Dollar

*"Nothing can stop the man with the right
mental attitude from achieving his goal;
nothing on earth can help the man
with the wrong mental attitude."*

— W. W. Ziege

Belief
Something or someone
you have confidence
and trust in.

BE
LIEF

Day 4

Belief: Trust It

Definition of *belief:*
Something or someone you have confidence and trust in.

Say It

As you speak the following phrases, believe and embrace them. Visualize yourself having what you state—possess it. Notice how your voice and body respond to each "I" statement:

- *I acknowledge the importance of believing in myself.*

- *I possess a strong internal belief in all that I do.*

- *I am who I believe I am.*

- *I am motivated by my beliefs. I demonstrate them through my words and deeds.*

- *I am transformed by the power of my beliefs.*

Believe It

Many things help program your beliefs, including books, newspapers, magazines, TV programs, radio broadcasts, the Internet, the things people say to you, and most important, the things you say to *yourself.*

For example, I vividly remember the day I ran home from kindergarten humiliated by my classmates' cruel taunts because I couldn't say my name without stuttering. For several years, I endured daily reprogramming from my speech therapists and my mother to build my confidence and trust in my ability. They repeatedly told me that one day I'd be able to say my name without tripping over my tongue. As a professional speaker, I thank God that I can now give an entire speech without stumbling over a word.

Thanks to my mom and all of my speech therapists and teachers, the belief was instilled in me that I could overcome this challenge. But in the end, they weren't the ones who transformed me— *I* transformed myself into a person who could speak without stammering because I believed what they told me. I incorporated their belief into my deepest being. I trusted that I could speak clearly and without hesitation or repetition. I believed it could happen, and it did.

Receive It

Eliminate all negative and toxic programming from your life immediately by replacing it with positive programming. Evaluate the phrases you hear yourself saying: Do they reflect a lack of belief? Do you hear yourself saying that you'll *try* to do something, rather than that you *will* do something? A friend of mine once sent me an e-mail announcing that for the new year, he was going to try to stop smoking. I zapped him with a reply that said, "Remember what Yoda said in *The Empire Strikes Back:* 'Try not. Do or do not. There is no try'!" If my friend believes that he'll only *try* to quit smoking, then he probably won't receive the gift of being a nonsmoker. When he truly *believes* he can quit, he will.

What would you like to receive in life? Write it down, relax, and bring it to you with your belief that it will happen.

Daily Quotes

"For the believer, there is no question; for the nonbeliever, there is no answer."

— Anonymous

"Believe that life is worth living, and your belief will help create the fact."

— William James

"Believe in something larger than yourself."

— Barbara Bush

chAL LENGE

Challenge
A demand;
a call to engage
in a contest or fight.

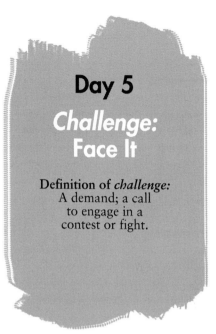

Day 5

Challenge:
Face It

Definition of *challenge:*
A demand; a call
to engage in a
contest or fight.

Say It

As you speak the following phrases, believe and embrace them. Visualize yourself having what you state—possess it. Notice how your voice and body respond to each "I" statement:

- *I acknowledge all challenges that I need to face in my life.*

- *I possess the power to overcome any challenges I face.*

- *I am able to overcome any challenges that come my way.*

- *I am stronger on the inside than the challenges I face on the outside.*

- *I am ready to tackle my challenges head-on.*

Believe It

Life is full of challenges. There's no limit to how many of them will come your way, so get ready, be ready, and stay ready. As I heard Garrison Keillor say on the radio recently, "Life is like war—if things get too quiet, you're losing." Of course he was making a joke, but the truth is that when the road gets too smooth, you have the tendency to become complacent. You won't be able to know what you're made of and grow stronger if everything in your life comes easily without bumps that challenge you to find new ways to resolve issues. If all of your relationships evolved perfectly and you never had any arguments, disagreements, or even differences of opinion, you'd never learn anything. You wouldn't be equipped to successfully handle difficult situations and, in essence, you'd be defeated. The fact of the matter is that challenges are a part of life, but God can use them to make you a better person by sharpening the qualities within you that are able to overcome those obstacles.

In the corporate world today, businesses want to increase profits, improve productivity, and reduce overhead. Many of my friends who work in this environment are called upon to do more with less—they're working longer hours with the same pay and fewer resources. Unfortunately, many of the companies they work for are being downsized or "right-sized"—so my friends can only face this type of challenge by having the right attitude and the ability to know they'll get through it. Almost everyone I know who ever lost a job looks back on the experience as a gift and a door to a better, greater opportunity.

Challenges break you out of your mold and help develop your character. And it's through them that life hands you new opportunities for success that you may never have experienced otherwise.

Receive It

How do you handle your challenges? Are you propelled to act by drawing on your inner strength and faith and focusing on what needs to be done? Or do you procrastinate, using food, shopping, or sleeping as easy escapes?

Instead of running away from them, you must face your challenges—when they come, see them as opportunities to grow. Receive your obstacles with warmth, appreciation, and love. Consider the Egyptians, the great builders of the pyramids. They would never have been able to erect those awesome structures without their perceived need for an eternal way to honor the kings and queens they highly esteemed. So receive the challenges that come your way and turn them into the great life lessons you're meant to learn. Build your own pyramid!

Daily Quotes

"Challenges—life is full of them; without them, how would you know and realize the awesome power that lives within you?"

— Keith D. Harrell

"A challenge is nothing but an opportunity turned upside down."

— Toni Malliet

"If you faint in the day of adversity, your strength is small."

— Proverbs 24:10

๑๏   ๑๏   ๑๏

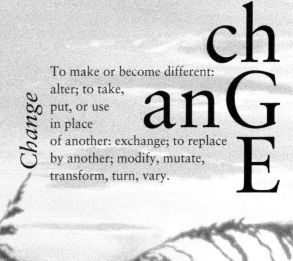

Change

ch
an
G
E

To make or become different:
alter; to take,
put, or use
in place
of another: exchange; to replace
by another; modify, mutate,
transform, turn, vary.

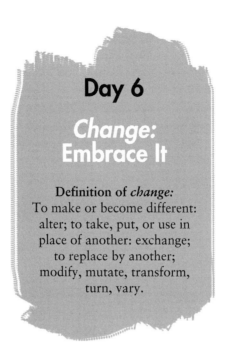

Day 6

Change:
Embrace It

Definition of *change:*
To make or become different:
alter; to take, put, or use in
place of another: exchange;
to replace by another;
modify, mutate, transform,
turn, vary.

Say It

As you speak the following phrases, believe and
embrace them. Visualize yourself having what you
state—possess it. Notice how your voice and body
respond to each "I" statement:

- *I acknowledge that I am a change
  embracer.*

- *I possess the skills needed to
  embrace change.*

- *I am willing to accept change in order to grow.*

- *I am changing on the inside, which brings about change on the outside.*

- *I am learning important lessons from the changes in my life.*

Believe It

Change is the essence of life—without it, we can't grow. A seed must absorb water, break open, and push forth a sprout in order to grow into a mighty oak . . . and human beings are no different. Change brings us the opportunity to be something even better than we were before.

When I considered leaving my hometown of Seattle to accept a job promotion in Atlanta, I first thought of the negatives: I'd be leaving my roots and my loved ones; I'd have to make new friends (or live a lonely life); I'd have to find a new place of worship, a new doctor, a new dentist, and a new place to live; and I felt apprehensive about moving to a part of the country where I hadn't spent much time, I didn't know the roads, and the traffic appeared to be three times worse than what I'd experienced in Seattle. Could I handle all that change?

I eventually wiped out my negative thoughts with positive ones: The promotion meant more money, more prestige, and more opportunity than ever before; the move would bring a new climate for me to experience; and leaving my old abode would give me a chance to clear out the things I no longer used or needed. I soon accepted that the changes were good, both personally and professionally. I faced change, embraced it, and welcomed it into my life. As a result, many doors opened up for me.

Receive It

Does an area in your life need to change? Do you want to lose weight, stop smoking, end a relationship, or move to a new location? Or has change thrust itself upon you? Have you lost a job, gone through a rift or separation of some sort, or experienced a life-changing injury or illness?

Determine what you need to embrace the new reality, whether it was thrust upon you or you decided to bring it about yourself. Identify whatever help you may need and go get it—seek out counseling with a minister or mental-health professional, find a support group of like-minded people dealing with similar situations, speak to your loved ones about the change, or read books on the subject.

In addition, to really accept that change, you'll need to modify your attitude. Here's how: Take some time to sit, meditate, and visualize how things will be once the event has taken place. See the positive aspects of the changes taking place, and welcome and invite into your life all the good things that will come about because of them.

Daily Quotes

"If you're not in a change mode, you're probably in a rut, and the only difference between a rut and a grave are the dimensions."

— Anonymous

"Change will either chain you to your past or free you to your future."

— Danielle Kennedy

"The only thing you can change is yourself, but sometimes that changes everything."

— Keith D. Harrell

Choice

The act of
choosing;
selection;
the power,
opportunity,
or right
to choose;
an option,
an alternative,
something
to choose
or select.

Choice

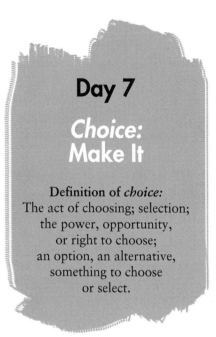

Day 7

Choice: Make It

Definition of *choice:*
The act of choosing; selection;
the power, opportunity,
or right to choose;
an option, an alternative,
something to choose
or select.

Say It

As you speak the following phrases, believe and embrace them. Visualize yourself having what you state—possess it. Notice how your voice and body respond to each "I" statement:

- *I acknowledge the importance of choice.*

- *I possess the ability to make the right choices for my life.*

- *I am making the right choices for my life.*

- *I am making choices that support the lifestyle that is right for me.*

- *I am making a choice to make this day an "attitude is everything" day.*

Believe It

The ability to make choices is one of the most powerful gifts God has given you. Think of how wonderful it is that you have the freedom to choose the direction you want your life to take. You have the ability to shape your future now, so if you want to experience success rather than failure, you've got to make choices that support that goal.

A man named William once told me about a choice he made when he was in his mid-20s. He'd been in the Navy, where he enjoyed being a dental technician, and he returned to civilian life to attend college on the GI Bill. When the time came to make a decision about his career, William had two job offers: The first, a delivery-truck driver, paid well, had impressive benefits, and promised promotions; the second opportunity involved a fledgling occupation no one had yet heard about, something called emergency medical technician (EMT). It didn't pay well, and there was a high possibility that the general public would never accept or respect it. Up to that point, ambulance drivers (as they had been called) were untrained—they simply threw injured people into station wagons and raced to the hospital.

William knew that money and promotions weren't his lifelong goals. Instead, his enjoyment came from being around medical personnel and helping others—in fact, he got chills at the prospect of saving lives and ministering to the injured. In the end, William became an EMT and later gained certification as a paramedic. He often delivered babies (although he never delivered packages), and he lived a gratifying life. He chose the right path for himself.

Receive It

Just like William, you must consider the final outcome you want to experience before you make a choice. William's passion and love for people propelled him into the career that made him the happiest—similarly, whenever *you* make a decision, ask yourself, "Are my choices moving me closer to or farther away from my goals? Are my choices honorable? How do these choices affect my loved ones?"

Life is just a series of decisions that will either make or break you. It's up to you to make the right choices so that you can experience the right outcome. You're a free moral agent—and freedom to choose your destiny is one of the greatest gifts God has given you. Ask Him to direct every choice you make, and have faith that He will guide you on the path to success.

Making beneficial choices doesn't have to be difficult. It just takes confidence in God. So know that you possess the knowledge to choose wisely. It's innately inside you—all you have to do is tap in to it and let it help you make the right decisions.

Daily Quotes

"Choosing to do nothing is still a choice."

— Reggie Green

*"The choices you made yesterday have impacted
your success today, while the choices you
will make today will impact
your success tomorrow."*

— Keith D. Harrell

*"In the long run we shape our lives and we
shape ourselves. The process never ends until
we die. And the choices we make are
ultimately our own responsibility."*

— Eleanor Roosevelt

Commitment
To be
responsible
for, or to,
something or
someone.
To pledge or
obligate yourself
to something
or someone.

CO
MMIT
MENT

Day 8

Commitment:
Honor It

Definition of *commitment:*
To be responsible for, or to,
something or someone.
To pledge or obligate
yourself to something
or someone.

Say It

As you speak the following phrases, believe and
embrace them. Visualize yourself having what you
state—possess it. Notice how your voice and body
respond to each "I" statement:

- *I acknowledge the importance of
  being committed.*

- *I possess the attitude to follow
  through on all my commitments.*

- *I am able to keep my commitments.*

- *I am remaining committed despite any challenges or obstacles.*

- *I am able to stay committed to my obligations so that I can achieve my desired outcome.*

Believe It

One of the reasons why you may be unable to see your vision come to pass is because you're not committed to it. Just like in a marriage in which a husband and wife pledge themselves to one another for life, you must make a similar dedication to what you want to see come to pass for yourself. Unfortunately, you may be so focused on your "big" dreams and goals that you fail to recognize that commitment starts with the "small" things. Before you'll be able to see success on a large scale, it's important to begin with the things you do every day—the habits you form now will determine your success later.

Recognizing the need to stay committed to something is the first step you need to take. For example, one of my goals awhile back was to see greater results in my spiritual life. When I recognized the need for more meaning in this area, I decided to do what it took to see that goal achieved. I became dedicated to improving that part of my life, and I stayed committed to my decision. I set my clock for the same time every morning and got up to pray for 15 minutes *every* day. I disciplined myself so consistently that getting up early to pray became a habit. Now I automatically get up at 4:30 every morning to do so. And because I stayed committed to my decision, I achieved my desired outcome.

The principle of commitment can apply to any area of your life that you'd like to change. From developing an exercise program, changing your eating habits, and getting to work on time, to improving your interpersonal relationships, it takes an unflinching devotion to your goal, regardless of how you feel. *This* is what will propel you to the results you're looking for.

Receive It

You can start by examining the small, everyday things that you'd like to make better. Pick one and make a 30-day commitment to do whatever is necessary to see change in that area. You may want to improve your personal relationships by going out of your way do nice things for others, or, if you want to drop a few extra pounds, you could commit to walking or jogging for 20 minutes a day. Start small and believe big.

By staying focused on the end result, you'll be more motivated to remain committed to your goal. So see yourself accomplishing the things you've set for yourself—*become* that final outcome in your mind, set your mind toward that goal, and refuse to abandon your commitment. Remember, seeing your vision come to pass depends on how determined you are to do what it takes to make it happen.

Daily Quotes

"We make decisions with our head; we make commitments with our heart."

— Anonymous

"If you don't make a total commitment to whatever you're doing, then you start looking to bail out the first time the boat starts leaking. It's tough enough getting that boat to shore with everybody rowing, let alone when a guy stands and starts putting his life jacket on."

— Lou Holtz

"Commitment: Doing the things that others won't do, in order to have the things that others won't have."

— Dr. Creflo Dollar

Communication

An act of effectively transmitting ideas; imparting, telling; the exchange of ideas, messages, or information, by speech, signals, and writing.

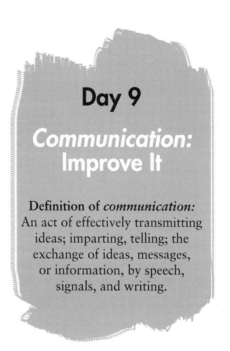

Day 9

Communication: Improve It

Definition of *communication:*
An act of effectively transmitting ideas; imparting, telling; the exchange of ideas, messages, or information, by speech, signals, and writing.

Say It

As you speak the following phrases, believe and embrace them. Visualize yourself having what you state—possess it. Notice how your voice and body respond to each "I" statement:

- *I acknowledge the importance of communication.*

- *I possess good communication skills.*

- *I am always communicating my thoughts through my words, deeds, and actions.*

- *I am an effective communicator, able to express myself whenever I need to.*

- *I am exchanging and sharing words of hope, love, and success.*

Believe It

As you enhance your speaking and listening skills, keep in mind that God gave you one mouth and two ears for a reason. Constantly talking without taking time to listen to others is not only irritating to the speaker, but it limits you, too. When you talk, you say only what you know; when you listen, you learn what others know.

More than 20 years ago, I decided to attend my first Toastmasters meeting in an effort to become a more confident speaker in front of my peers at work. Today I speak to audiences of thousands, and I still use the fundamentals of public speaking I learned then: Establish good eye contact, maintain a relaxed demeanor, speak clearly, and express the appropriate emotions and enthusiasm to convey ideas.

To enhance her sales, my friend Beverly took a course called Assertive Listening. Every evening after class, she went home and practiced her new skills. Whenever her child spoke, Beverly would ask a probing question to get more information. With her husband, she'd repeat what he said to show him that she heard clearly before she'd respond. To her surprise, as Beverly practiced better communication, not only did her sales pick up, but she also improved relations with her family.

Effectively being able to communicate with others is essential to your success. From your business and career to your interpersonal relationships, you have to know how to balance speaking and listening, as too much of one or the other will prove to be hindrances to your communication skills.

Receive It

The next time you talk to someone, pay attention to yourself: Do you monopolize the conversation, barely allowing the other person to get a word in? As the other person speaks, are you thinking of what you're going to say next, or are you paying attention to what he or she is saying? If you normally plan your next comment instead of quietly and carefully listening, you're missing the vital information the other person's trying to tell you because you're so busy trying to figure out how you're going to respond.

Begin to practice the fundamentals of communication by paying close attention while others are speaking. Ask clarifying questions, such as: "When you say [such and such], do you mean [so and so]?" or "So you say you [fill in the blank]?" When you actively listen and respond to others when they're speaking, you improve your relationship with them *and* gain valuable information that can help you make decisions later.

You may also want to consider enrolling in a communications course to help you in this area, as my friend Beverly did. Not only will you develop as a person, but you'll also improve your relationships and your career. Welcome and enjoy the benefits of a new level of communication.

Daily Quotes

"He who does not understand your silence will probably not understand your words."

— Elbert Hubbard

"It takes two to speak the truth— one to speak and another to hear."

— Henry David Thoreau

"It's just as important to say what you mean as it is to mean what you say."

— Anonymous

Completion

Entire,
full,
intact,
integral,
perfect,
whole.

comPle
TION

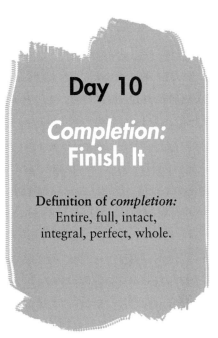

Day 10

Completion: Finish It

Definition of *completion*:
Entire, full, intact,
integral, perfect, whole.

Say It

As you speak the following phrases, believe and
embrace them. Visualize yourself having what you
state—possess it. Notice how your voice and body
respond to each "I" statement:

- *I acknowledge the importance of
  getting things done.*

- *I possess the ability to finish what
  I start.*

- *I am complete in all I do.*

- *I am complete—worthy, whole, and perfect in God's sight.*

- *I am willing to do whatever it takes to finish what I started, and to bring all unfinished tasks to completion.*

Believe It

Several years ago, *Parade* magazine carried a story about Olympic marathon runner John Stephen Akhwari from Tanzania. During the 1968 Olympic games, Akhwari was the last runner to finish the grueling 26-mile race. His leg was bloodied and bandaged because he had fallen and severely injured his knee. When he painfully hobbled across the finish line, a reporter approached him and asked why he hadn't quit. He said, "My country did not send me [here] to start the race. They sent me to finish."

Akhwari stayed focused on the end result—finishing the race—rather than the fact that his injury ruined his chances of winning. If he'd given his attention to the challenge rather than the finish line, he would have given up on the race. You must have the same attitude when it comes to completing those things you've set your mind to accomplish. Even when it looks impossible or negative situations arise, make a decision to complete the task at hand. It's not enough to set goals for yourself, if you fail to complete the steps necessary to achieve those goals. Many people have dreams and visions that never materialize because they're not committed to completing them, and it isn't uncommon for people to start things that they never finish. Don't let distractions, complacency, and hardships keep *you* from success: Commit to completion in everything you undertake.

Receive It

It's critical that you do your research and understand exactly what it will take to complete your tasks—you need to be very detail oriented in coming up with an effective plan. Write down all the things you'll need to do, and dedicate yourself to seeing your projects and goals through to the end. For example, if your goal is to lose a certain amount of weight and achieve a certain size, you know that there are some things that you're going to have to implement in order to see that goal come to pass. You'll need to come up with an exercise plan that incorporates cardiovascular and weight training. You'll also have to rethink your eating habits and make changes in your diet. Even when you don't feel like continuing, you'll have to set your will to finish what you start.

If you're having a difficult time completing a task, stay focused, be resourceful, and get help if necessary. Seek the support of friends and family who can encourage you when you want to give up. Much of the challenge is a mental one—being able to overcome the temptation to quit. Getting a visual picture of the end result is critical to keep you going. See yourself finishing your assignment with excellence. Try to envision how it will feel once you're done. And be convinced in your heart that completion is the key to success.

Daily Quotes

*"What we call the beginning is often the end,
And to make an end is to make a beginning.
The end is where we start from."*

— T. S. Eliot

*"A thing that cannot be accomplished
should never be undertaken."*

— African (Yoruba) proverb

*"The completion of one task signals
the beginning of something new."*

— Anonymous

Confidence

Reliance or trust;
a trusting relationship;
a feeling of self-assurance;
belief or faith.

Day 11

Confidence: Hold On to It

Definition of *confidence*:
Reliance or trust;
a trusting relationship;
a feeling of self-assurance;
belief or faith.

Say It

As you speak the following phrases, believe and embrace them. Visualize yourself having what you state—possess it. Notice how your voice and body respond to each "I" statement:

- *I acknowledge the importance of having confidence.*

- *I possess the confidence to do all things.*

- *I have the confidence to overcome any adversity in my life.*

- *I am confident in my ability to achieve my goals.*

- *I am bold and full of courage. I face every situation with confidence.*

Believe It

Bobbie was the typical mother: She held a full-time job; kept up with the housework, shopping, and laundry; and shuttled her son to soccer practices and games several times a week. Her duties as a soccer mom included providing refreshments to the team every couple of weeks. Needless to say, she was a very busy person.

As the summer grew longer, Bobbie watched the team morale drop as the heat took its toll. Week after week, her son's team lost, and their confidence went downhill. Parents discussed what they might do to help improve the situation, but they could only cheer from the sidelines and hope that their children would somehow miraculously feel better about themselves.

On one of the days that Bobbie was supposed to provide the refreshments, she cut some oranges into bite-sized segments and then reached into her freezer to get some orange juice. Unfortunately, she suddenly realized that she'd forgotten to buy any. She only had grape juice—and no one had *ever* brought grape juice as a refreshment! Yet with little time to spare, Bobbie added water to the frozen grape juice, filled the pitchers, loaded the car with her son and his equipment (plus the snacks), and headed for the soccer field. Fortunately, they got there in the nick of time.

Once again, Bobbie and the other parents watched the kids dragging their feet, looking sad and lacking confidence. It was clear that they weren't in good spirits, and the score reflected their feelings. Bobbie figured that morale would sink even lower when the kids discovered they didn't have their customary orange juice to drink at halftime.

As soon as the referee's whistle blew, the dejected boys and girls rushed over for refreshments . . . and an idea struck Bobbie. She gathered the kids around her, and before she poured them their drinks, she announced, "I want you all to know that I didn't bring the usual juice for refreshments today—instead, I brought you Super Juice! Super Juice is absolutely guaranteed to make you play and feel better. Drink up, and then go out there and win the game!"

The kids watched her pour the purple juice into their cups, and it wasn't long before they got into the spirit. Several raised their cups and said, "Here's to Super Juice!" By the time the game started again, all the kids were laughing, cheering, and feeling confident.

Did they win? You bet they did—and from that day forward, the team insisted that all the other mothers bring Super Juice for refreshments every time. What changed? The only thing different with these kids was their level of confidence. They believed that the juice would energize them and make them play better, and, therefore, they *were* energized—and they won. It wasn't until the soccer team was able to put its confidence in something that it was able to overcome the negativity that it faced.

Receive It

The greatest challenges to your confidence come when you're facing a situation that *looks* impossible. When this happens, you must tap in to the unseen force of self-assurance so that you can press beyond supposed limits. It's not a matter of what things look like on the outside—the key is to recognize what you have working on the *inside*. Confidence is often the missing link to seeing yourself accomplish the impossible. You just have to believe that you have what it takes to be successful, and don't back down from your capable stance.

You are in control of your thoughts. If you choose to believe you have confidence—that you're energized with Super Juice—then you will be. The next time you face a big challenge, take a deep breath and fill your heart with the belief that you have Super Juice running through your veins. Build your confidence by reflecting on those things you've already accomplished. If you did it once, you can certainly do it again.

Today, receive the confidence you deserve— and you'll find that you always had it within you.

Daily Quotes

*"He who has lost confidence
can lose nothing more."*

— Anonymous

*"Confidence is contagious.
So is lack of confidence."*

— Vince Lombardi

"To be confident is to act in faith."

— Bernard Bynion

desire
To hope or wish
for ardently;
to ask for: request;
a request or petition.

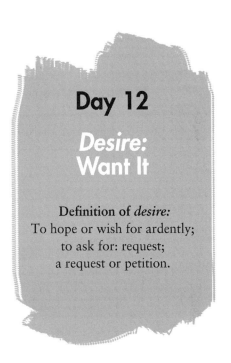

Day 12

Desire: Want It

Definition of *desire:*
To hope or wish for ardently;
to ask for: request;
a request or petition.

Say It

As you speak the following phrases, believe and embrace them. Visualize yourself having what you state—possess it. Notice how your voice and body respond to each "I" statement:

- *I acknowledge my internal desire as a driving force that will help me succeed.*

- *I possess the desire to do all things.*

- *I am building a stronger level of desire each day to do the things I need to do to succeed.*

- *I am able to stay motivated by my strong desire to excel.*

- *I am renewed by my desire to achieve.*

Believe It

Desire is a key force that will propel you to success. God placed this force inside of you so that you would constantly have fuel to run on, in order to be successful. It's one of the things that will keep you going when you want to quit. When your desire to accomplish your goals is strong enough, you won't let anything stop you. Here's an example of what I mean.

As a preteen, Terry was active in sports and enjoyed playing soccer, basketball, and tennis. She was on the swim team and was a member of the cheerleading squad; in addition, she took ballet and tap-dancing lessons, as she had a strong desire to become a professional dancer one day. Yet when she was 12, the unthinkable happened: Terry was in a serious car accident that broke her back and injured her spinal column. Doctors, nurses, physical therapists, and family members prepared her for life in a wheelchair, telling her she'd never walk again.

For many people, this experience would have quenched their desire for success. Upon receiving such news, it would be easy to throw in the towel on life and give up. But Terry's desires didn't go away just because she received a bad report from the doctors. Did she stop wanting to be active, to play sports and dance? No, because her desires were an integral part of her being. Terry quickly learned how to deal with the challenge, and she made sure that she gained a great deal of upper-body strength in order to help her move around better in her manual wheelchair. Day by day, she kept on going, always having the desire to do more and holding on to her dreams of being an athlete or performer.

At the time of her accident, Terry lived in a small town in Tennessee that didn't offer much in terms of recreation for people using wheelchairs, so she waited until she was old enough to attend college. She chose a school in Atlanta because she knew more opportunities would be available to her in a larger city. Sure enough, not only did Terry graduate from college with a double major (both theater and communications), but she also found a physically integrated dance company that employed dancers with and without disabilities. With her strong upper body and even stronger desire, Terry tried out and won a spot in the troupe. Today she performs as a dancer . . . and she gets paid to do it, too.

Terry's story is proof that a strong desire to succeed, regardless of the circumstances, will ensure success. Nothing can stop someone who has a deep-seated wish to accomplish his or her goals.

Receive It

Desire is the fire that brings enthusiasm to a boil, the power behind all great successes. Desire transcends obstacles and barriers and brings you what you want when you spend time cultivating it and then stepping out on it in faith.

You can begin to develop your God-given desires by spending a little time each day seeing, feeling, expressing, enjoying, and building what you want. Look at images of what you want to see come to pass. Bring that desire to the boiling point so that you can see it manifesting in your life easily and quickly. Fuel yourself with the belief that your desires are the bubbling, churning, burning steam engines that take you where you want to go. Celebrate and honor your desires, and follow where they lead you, for they'll take you further than you've ever gone before.

Remember, desire takes you beyond limitations—it ignores challenges and setbacks and helps you plow forward.

Daily Quotes

"He who desires but acts not is simply unwilling to play the hand he's been dealt."

— Anonymous

"Desire—it's the D-factor. It's the force on the inside that is displayed by an unstoppable action to never, never, never give up."

— Keith D. Harrell

"Delight thyself in the Lord; and He shall give thee the desires of thine heart."

— Psalms 37:4

෧෨ ෧෨ ෧෨

DES
tiNY

destiny
Fate;
a predetermined
or inevitable
course of
events.

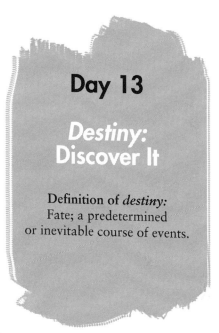

Day 13

Destiny: Discover It

Definition of *destiny*:
Fate; a predetermined
or inevitable course of events.

Say It

As you speak the following phrases, believe and embrace them. Visualize yourself having what you state—possess it. Notice how your voice and body respond to each "I" statement:

- *I acknowledge my destiny.*

- *I possess the ability to fulfill my destiny.*

- *I am fulfilling my destiny.*

- *I am committed to my destiny.*

- *I am here to make a difference and was created for a special plan and purpose.*

Believe It

God wants you to discover your destiny—He doesn't want you to wander aimlessly through life, not knowing what you were put on Earth to do. Most likely, you already have a clue as to what your destiny is, but you're allowing obstacles to keep you from fulfilling it. On the other hand, sometimes obstacles can be viewed as "spiritual bumpers" that God is using to steer you in the right direction for your divine destiny. If you continue to pursue the path that's wrong for you, you'll never get to your destination in life. At the same time, you can benefit from the experiences you have along the way to help you gain valuable skills that will benefit you later on.

In college, I thought I knew my destiny—to play in the NBA. At 6'7", I was on the starting lineup of my basketball team all four years, was captain three years in a row, and averaged a little more than 16 points a game in my senior year. And, most important, I had a passion for the game. When the NBA didn't draft me, I realized that even though a basketball career wasn't part of my destiny, the knowledge I'd gleaned from my experiences has helped me develop many skills I needed to be successful today. Basketball taught me self-discipline, teamwork, and the importance of having a game plan. Similarly, all of *your* life experiences can become stepping-stones to your final destination.

Receive It

Think of what you want to do, for whom, for what purpose, and how you're going to do it. Then get a plan together to determine what you want to ultimately get out of your goals. Planning is critically important when you're fulfilling your destiny, so carefully calculate the steps you must take to realize your dreams. Factor in the extra things you may need to do to be the best at what you've been called to be. For example, maybe you need to take a class or read books that will help give you the extra edge and information you need to succeed. Examine your strengths and weaknesses, as well as the gifts and talents you've been blessed with, which are all clues to God's divine plan for your life. When challenges, setbacks, or negative thoughts get in the way, consider them as mere pebbles in your path. Even when people try to block your progress, walk in love toward them and trust that the path you're on is true. Just keep stepping over anything that gets in the way of your fulfilling your destiny.

Destiny is the path and direction God has prepared for you. All the experiences you've had in life—both good and bad—have happened in order to help propel you into your ultimate outcome. When you allow vision, faith, commitment, and action to come together, you'll be able to successfully reach your goals and fulfill your destiny.

Daily Quotes

*"Life is what happens to you while you're busy
making other plans."*

— John Lennon

*"Destiny is not a matter of chance; it is a matter
of choice. It is not a thing to be waited for,
it is a thing to be achieved."*

— William Jennings Bryan

*"[When it comes to destiny], if you aren't going
all the way, why go at all?"*

— Joe Namath

enthusiasm
Intense
feeling
for
a
subject
or
cause;
eagerness;
zeal.

enthuS
IASM

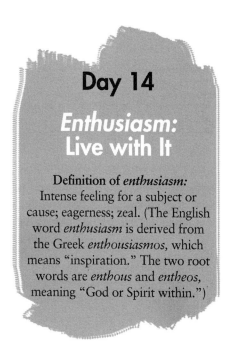

Day 14

Enthusiasm: Live with It

Definition of *enthusiasm:*
Intense feeling for a subject or cause; eagerness; zeal. (The English word *enthusiasm* is derived from the Greek *enthousiasmos*, which means "inspiration." The two root words are *enthous* and *entheos*, meaning "God or Spirit within.")

Say It

As you speak the following phrases, believe and embrace them. Visualize yourself having what you state—possess it. Notice how your voice and body respond to each "I" statement:

- *I acknowledge that I am enthusiastic.*

- *I possess enthusiasm.*

- *I am enthusiastic about the possibilities that this day will bring.*

- *I am excited about life and the difference I can make in the lives of others.*

- *I am enthusiastic and leave a lasting positive impression on everyone I meet.*

Believe It

Enthusiasm can be defined by the last four letters of the word: I Am Seriously Motivated. Communicating commitment, determination, and spirit, enthusiasm is infectious and will affect everyone around you. And it will keep *you* motivated as well.

During my talks, I sometimes divide participants into two groups. I tell them we're having an enthusiasm contest, and I want the first group to generate the most noise it can, while the second group waits for its turn. Without fail, the second group is always the loudest, for one simple reason: Enthusiasm is contagious. But don't take it from me—go to any sporting event and watch the cheerleaders. Their pep gets the crowd excited, and the crowd's exuberance then spurs the athletes on to perform their best.

Trust that enthusiasm works: The applicant with the most enthusiasm usually wins the job; the dog with the most enthusiasm gets the treat; and the person with the most enthusiasm boosts him- or herself to success. Enthusiasm is a telltale sign that you believe in yourself and what you're trying to accomplish—and when you're this convinced, other people will be, too.

Receive It

Children innately have enthusiasm. Watch them get excited over a new toy, a tasty treat, or a game. The odd thing is that you don't lose your enthusiasm as you grow older—instead, you bury it. You pile layers of stress, doubt, obligations, resentments, and other useless preoccupations on top of your zeal until it appears to be snuffed out. It's still there, though—you just need to uncover it. Act as if you have it, and soon your real eagerness will bubble up through the mire and appear on the surface.

You can make every day an "attitude is everything" day just by allowing it to be so. Draw enthusiasm to you and share it with others. Unmask your excitement for life, let it glow, and allow it to bring you whatever you want. Never let the kid in you die.

Daily Quotes

"We act as though comfort and luxury were the chief requirements in life, when all that we need to make us really happy is something to be enthusiastic about."

— Charles Kingsley

"If you aren't fired with enthusiasm, you will be fired with enthusiasm."

— Vince Lombardi

"The world belongs to the energetic."

— Ralph Waldo Emerson

෧෨ ෧෨ ෧෨

excellence
Exceptionally good, fine;
first-class, first-rate; superior; of
great value or worth.

EXCEL
lence

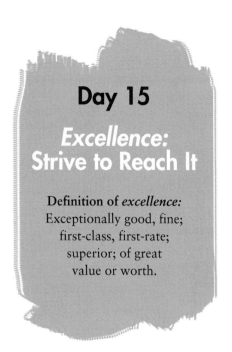

Day 15

Excellence:
Strive to Reach It

Definition of *excellence:*
Exceptionally good, fine;
first-class, first-rate;
superior; of great
value or worth.

Say It

As you speak the following phrases, believe and embrace them. Visualize yourself having what you state—possess it. Notice how your voice and body respond to each "I" statement:

- *I acknowledge excellence as a standard for my life.*

- *I possess excellence in all that I do.*

- *I am a living example of God's excellence.*

- *I am living a life of excellence.*

- *I am striving for excellence minute by minute, day by day.*

Believe It

Anita had waited tables, worked at fast-food establishments, and held a few other low-paying jobs, but she knew that she was getting nowhere in life. She had no training or special expertise that set her apart, yet she wanted to work for herself and build a business where her hard work would be repaid.

Anita realized that she could clean houses for a living, but she wondered what she could do to set herself apart from other housekeepers. Instead of starting just another housecleaning company, she decided that her service would be a few steps above anything anyone else did. For example, when she met with a client for the first time, Anita asked what extra chores she might do regularly. She inquired whether or not the client wanted the refrigerator emptied and cleaned once a month. Would he or she like the deck swept regularly or the tops of the cabinets dusted every week?

Anita wrote down all the extra little chores she promised her clients, and then she did them. And then she took her excellence one step further. If she noticed that a client's linen closet had gotten messy, she'd take all the towels and sheets out, refold them, and put them all back in neat stacks (without even telling the client); if she saw a fixture that needed cleaning, she cleaned it; and she looked for other little tasks that made her service better than all the others.

Soon Anita's clients bragged about her to their friends, and her business grew so large that she had to hire assistants to help her. Excellence in what she did had set her apart from the competition.

Receive It

Excellence is an attitude. Many times it's tempting to take the easier route and do only what's necessary to get a job done. Unfortunately, even though this way of doing things may be faster, all too often you end up sacrificing the quality of the job you're doing.

Maintaining a standard of excellence in your life is essential. Examine the little things that you do and ask yourself if there's any way you could do them in a more outstanding way—perhaps it's meticulously cleaning your house or your car or going the extra mile at work. If you maintain a high standard in your personal life, that same spirit will carry over into other areas of your life.

The next time you face a task or take on a new job, look for ways you can stand out. How can you do the job even better than those before you or those who do the same thing? Write down those little tasks that make a big difference. When you do them, you'll see that they add up to excellence that will set you apart and put you on the right track for success. Incorporate an A-plus standard into *everything* you do, and watch your life change.

Daily Quotes

"The keynote of progress, we should remember, is not merely doing away with what is bad; it is replacing the best with something better."

— Edward A. Filene

"To serve with excellence is to work above the expectations of others."

— Keith D. Harrell

"Whatever is worth doing at all is worth doing well."

— Philip Dormer Stanhope, Earl of Chesterfield

faith

Trust.
Belief.
Belief and
trust
in God.
A set of
principles
or beliefs.
Confident
belief in
the truth;
value,
or trust-
worthiness
of a person,
idea, or thing.

faith

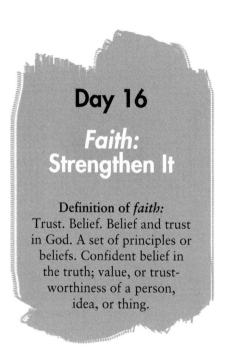

Day 16

Faith:
Strengthen It

Definition of *faith:*
Trust. Belief. Belief and trust
in God. A set of principles or
beliefs. Confident belief in
the truth; value, or trust-
worthiness of a person,
idea, or thing.

Say It

As you speak the following phrases, believe and
embrace them. Visualize yourself having what you
state—possess it. Notice how your voice and body
respond to each "I" statement:

- *I acknowledge the importance
  of living my life by faith.*

- *I possess faith.*

- *I am relying on my faith to do all things. I expect great things to happen in my life.*

- *I am anticipating a miracle.*

- *I am walking and living by faith.*

Believe It

Faith is the foundation for the things you hope for. The stronger your faith, the greater the possibility of seeing your desires become a reality. For example, several years ago I was diagnosed with blood clots in both my legs, but I had faith that God would heal me. While I was in the hospital being treated, my doctor explained the seriousness of the condition, saying that if even one of the clots broke free and went to my brain, it could kill me. I *knew* God wasn't going to let such a thing happen to me—I had faith that the treatments I received would dissolve the clots and I'd be restored to perfect health. My belief kept me from worrying about the outcome of the situation or asking, "Why me?" Instead of getting depressed about what was happening, I relied on my faith. It kept me going each day, in total trust that all would be well. Because I absolutely knew that God would heal me, I'm perfectly fine today.

Faith will pull you through any situation you're facing. I know that whenever I'm confronted with adversity, it's my faith that enables me to overcome by causing my belief to be unshakable.

Receive It

To strengthen your faith, read, study, and listen to spiritual materials and live by trusting in God, believing that everything will work out the way it should. Take time to sit in meditation or prayer every morning and evening so that your mind and spirit can calm down. Focus on the goodness of God. In your morning quiet time, feel the trust in your heart and allow it to become a part of your soul, letting it spring from deep within you. Know that all is well. Have confidence in the fact that the universe works perfectly and in divine order—everything is happening according to the divine plan.

Structure your day in the way you'd like it to unfold, and believe that it will be so. Then, take five minutes or more to pray or meditate every evening, and reflect on all that happened that day. Be thankful for the blessings that came to you and for the ones that have yet to come your way. Be grateful for your health, your life, and your ability to improve every day that you're on this planet. Faith is nothing without gratitude, so be sure to always be thankful for what you *already* have.

It's also important to take the necessary steps to see the manifestation of your faith come to pass, so find out what you need to do to set things in motion. Become an active participant in making your faith real.

Daily Quotes

*"Now faith is the substance of things hoped for,
the evidence of things not seen."*

— Hebrews 11:1

*"The way to see by faith is to shut
the eye of reason."*

— Benjamin Franklin

*"I believe in the sun, even if it isn't shining.
I believe in love even when I am alone.
I believe in God even when He is silent."*

— Anonymous

෩ ෩ ෩

GOal

goal   A purpose: objective;
the finish line of a race.

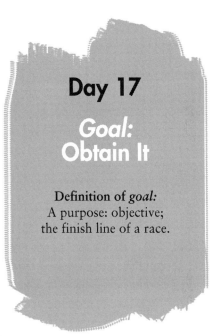

Day 17

Goal:
Obtain It

Definition of *goal:*
A purpose: objective;
the finish line of a race.

Say It

As you speak the following phrases, believe and embrace them. Visualize yourself having what you state—possess it. Notice how your voice and body respond to each "I" statement:

- *I acknowledge the importance of setting goals for my life.*

- *I possess the power to achieve my goals.*

- *I am working on my goals daily.*

- *I am committed to reaching all of my goals.*

- *I am a goal-setter: I write them down, I review them, and I obtain them.*

Believe It

You can achieve your goals, regardless of your circumstances. For instance, I recently read about a 73-year-old woman who graduated from college. Her age didn't bother her—she simply set a goal to become a college graduate, and she achieved it.

A similar example comes from Mike Rothberg, founder of Corporate Finance Associates, a world-wide business brokerage firm. Mike saw many associates join his business with enthusiasm, but few ever fulfilled their initial promise.

When Mike's young stepson, Jim, wanted to enter the business, Mike warned him that he'd need to have enough money to live on for the first few years until the money started to come in. Jim said he'd be fine, and he opened up an office in Colorado. The first year, Jim closed a deal or two and made a decent income. The next year, Jim's office performed even better, and his success continued. Practically every month, Jim closed deals that Mike never thought possible.

One day Mike met with Jim and asked his secret. The young man pulled a thin, worn slip of paper from his wallet. He unfolded it and read the following words: "In the first year, make $50,000. In the second year, make $100,000. Make 50 percent more each year. Before the tenth year, buy the business." Mike looked puzzled, so Jim explained, "You have to know your goals in order to achieve them. I write mine down and keep them with me. I read this piece of paper every day—that's how I reach my goals."

Mike stammered, "B-but if you do what that paper says, you're going to buy me out!"

Nodding, Jim said, "You're already past retirement age, while I'm the young blood this company needs. I'm learning all I can about the business. You may as well plan to retire sometime in the near future, because I reach every goal I write down and keep in my wallet."

Sure enough, Jim made Mike an offer in a few years—he'd met his goal, while Mike stayed on as a consultant for several years afterward. Everyone benefited from the arrangement.

You're never too old or too young to go after your dreams. It may sound simplistic to say that all you have to do to reach your goals is to write them down, but it's true. Write down your objectives, and give yourself a deadline for each one. Keep the paper near you and read it once a day. This technique has worked for Jim and many others—now it's time to put it to work for you.

Receive It

Write down a goal that you want to achieve in the next 40 days, and then set up mini-goals, or the steps that you need to take to achieve the larger goal. Put deadlines beside each one—and in 40 days, celebrate your accomplishment.

Daily Quotes

*"Set short-term goals and you'll win games.
Set long-term goals and you'll win the
championship!"*

— Anonymous

"Aim at nothing and you'll succeed."

— Anonymous

*"Concentrate on finding your goal,
then concentrate on reaching it."*

— Colonel Michael Friedman

GRATitude

gratitude
Thankfulness; appreciation;
the abundant blessing
of being thankful.

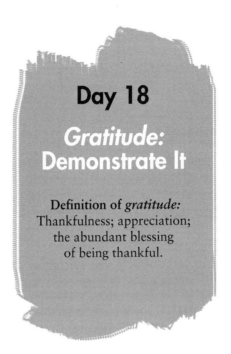

Day 18

Gratitude:
Demonstrate It

Definition of *gratitude:*
Thankfulness; appreciation;
the abundant blessing
of being thankful.

Say It

As you speak the following phrases, believe and embrace them. Visualize yourself having what you state—possess it. Notice how your voice and body respond to each "I" statement:

- *I acknowledge the importance of having an attitude of gratitude.*

- *I possess an attitude of gratitude.*

- *I am grateful for this day. I live with an attitude of thankfulness.*

- *I am abundantly blessed.*

- *I am thankful for my victories, and I rejoice during my setbacks; each provides an opportunity to remind myself how blessed I am.*

Believe It

Having gratitude helps you make every day an "attitude is everything" day. I mean, can you even count all that you have to be grateful for? Be thankful that you woke up this morning and are alive. Listen to the birds sing outside the window—appreciate that nature brings you delights. Give thanks to God for your loved ones, and appreciate the food you eat. Be grateful that you're on your way to great success.

My acquaintance Paul and his wife found themselves on the verge of bankruptcy after their craft business failed. Paul knew he had to leave the business he loved and get a job he probably wouldn't enjoy, and he felt bitter that he'd endured a major setback. However, his wife didn't seem to feel this way at all. She'd been attending classes based on *A Course in Miracles,* and she'd learned that in each setback lies a lesson, and everything is temporary.

Paul's wife took him to the classes, and he came away with a message that pulled him through: "I found out I needed to live with an attitude of gratitude," he says. "After all, I had my health. I had the ability to get a job, and I could also find a job I'd enjoy. With the help of a credit counselor, we were able to keep our home, so we had a nice place to live. We owned two cars, so we could get to our new jobs. We had food on the table, and we were off on a new journey—that was all. It wasn't a defeat, it was an opportunity. Now I get up every morning, thankful to be so filled with gifts and blessings, and I look forward to the next challenge."

Maintaining an attitude of gratitude is the key to seeing more of God's blessings manifest in your life. Celebrate the gifts and talents that you've been given. Be thankful for the little things, and expect more goodness to come your way.

Receive It

Any day above ground is a good day. The fact that you have warm blood flowing through your veins and breath in your body is reason to celebrate. A lot of people didn't make it that far, so take a deep breath and give thanks. You can take practical steps to put an attitude of gratitude in motion: For the next several days, write down at least five things daily that you're grateful for. You'll soon realize that the list is never-ending! There are so many things to thank God for that every day becomes an opportunity to acknowledge and receive more blessings.

The more you begin to live a thankful life, the more you'll begin to see your blessings multiply. Make a conscious effort to thank as many people as you can today for anything, no matter how big or small. Watch the transformation that happens in your life when you continually maintain an attitude of gratitude, one that says, "Thank You, God."

Daily Quotes

*"God gave you a gift of 86,400 seconds today.
Have you used one to say 'thank you'?"*

— William A. Ward

"Joy is the simplest form of gratitude."

— William A. Ward

*"When you wake up and there is no chalk
outline around your body, that's a good day
to embrace an attitude of gratitude."*

— Anonymous

෧෨ ෧෨ ෧෨

humility

Absence of pride. Cheerful submission to others.
The state or quality of being humble in
mind and spirit. A sincere commitment
to serve others; to separate oneself
from pretense and pride.

hum
ILITY

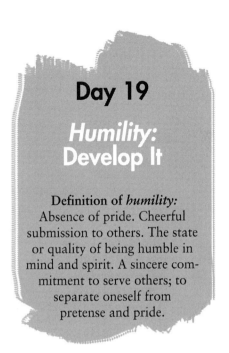

Day 19

Humility: Develop It

Definition of *humility*:
Absence of pride. Cheerful submission to others. The state or quality of being humble in mind and spirit. A sincere commitment to serve others; to separate oneself from pretense and pride.

Say It

As you speak the following phrases, believe and embrace them. Visualize yourself having what you state—possess it. Notice how your voice and body respond to each "I" statement:

- *I acknowledge my spirit of humility.*

- *I possess and embrace the attitude of humility.*

- *I am humbled by the blessings I receive from God.*

- *I am humble in all that I do.*

- *I am always humble with others.*

Believe It

I'm sure you've encountered arrogant, conceited people in your life. Do you remember how they made you feel? Probably not very good, and it's doubtful that you were looking forward to running into them again. On the opposite end of the spectrum, humility is pleasing to others. You can never offend anyone by being modest. In addition, maintaining a humble attitude keeps you from having an exaggerated opinion of yourself. It shields you from becoming prideful and keeps you focused on others, rather than concentrating on yourself and your abilities.

The first time I spoke in front of my peers at a National Speakers Association conference, I really wanted to impress them. I believed that everyone there had more experience and possessed better speaking skills than I did. In an effort to wow everyone, I operated out of my own self-interest rather than focusing on the needs of my audience. I prepared a speech that I hoped would knock their socks off, forgetting that if you work too hard to make an impression, you set yourself up for ridicule. But despite my error, the warm response and acceptance of my contemporaries humbled me. From then on, I made a decision to always consider my audience and keep my ego out of the way. That experience taught me how to be modest. Humility has made me a much better speaker and a much better man.

Receive It

Ask any comedian what makes for good humor, and you'll find out that embarrassing others is number one on their list. When someone else is embarrassed, the onlookers often get a good belly laugh, and the comedian looks good in their eyes. How can you turn *your* most humbling experience into laughter? Think back on a time when you were trying too hard to impress someone—did it work? You may have even made the other party giggle at your failed attempts at getting his or her attention. How would you do things differently now, knowing that humility is much more impressive than arrogance?

Where there is patience and humility, there is neither strife nor anger. Humility can't walk with ego, which stands for <u>E</u>dging <u>G</u>od <u>O</u>ut. To be humble, you've got to get *yourself* out of the way and focus on other people. Once you start taking the attention away from yourself, you'll realize that your needs aren't the only ones that count, and you'll be able to meet the needs of others more effectively.

In your quiet time, think about your most humbling experience. Why was it so humbling? What did you learn from it? Now that you know how much more effective humility is than pride when it comes to impressing other people, find out how you can bring that attitude into more of your daily interactions.

Daily Quotes

"For everyone who exalts himself shall be humbled, and he who humbles himself shall be exalted."

— Luke 14:11

"A man wrapped up in himself makes a very small bundle."

— Benjamin Franklin

"The proud man counts his newspaper clippings—the humble man his blessings."

— Bishop Fulton J. Sheen

integrity

integrity

Strict adherence to
a standard of value or
conduct; personal honesty
and independence;
completeness; unity.

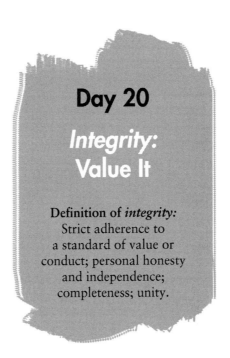

Day 20

Integrity:
Value It

Definition of *integrity:*
Strict adherence to
a standard of value or
conduct; personal honesty
and independence;
completeness; unity.

Say It

As you speak the following phrases, believe and embrace them. Visualize yourself having what you state—possess it. Notice how your voice and body respond to each "I" statement:

- *I acknowledge integrity as one of the core values for my life.*

- *I possess integrity in all that I do.*

- *I am credible. I always keep my word.*

- *I am a person of integrity.*

- *I am respectful of others. I always conduct myself in a respectful manner.*

Believe It

Integrity will take you further than any other value you possess. People may forget many of the things you do in your life, but they'll remember if you lived your life with integrity. They'll certainly remember if you don't. We've all seen the headlines of disgraced politicians who, when running for office, made an implicit pledge to be honest and truthful. Yet when the truth about their underhanded dealings was revealed, they lost face, lost elections, and often lost their freedom by going to prison.

Sometimes your desire to do something else after you've made a commitment tempts you to compromise your integrity. I was faced with such a situation when I made plans to attend my 20th high school reunion. I was all set to go, and then the committee changed the date at the last minute. Unfortunately, I had a business engagement on the new date, and my customer expected me to honor my commitment. I went back and forth between my choices—I wanted to attend the reunion, but if I'd gone, I wouldn't have fully enjoyed it because I would have known I'd let a client down.

I followed through with my promise to the client, but I missed the reunion I'd really wanted to attend. At first, my only consolation was the hopeful thought that my classmates would hold future reunions, but the lasting consolation came from knowing that I'd fulfilled a pledge to a client, and that promise came before my own pleasure. So I did the right thing. My desire to maintain a high standard of personal integrity for myself and in the eyes of others is what kept me grounded in my commitment.

Receive It

Integrity is the platform from which you should build all your relationships—with friends, relatives, clients, spouses, children, colleagues, and even animals. Never compromise by cheating and doing wrong, because in the end, it will destroy you. Integrity has to be what fuels your life. If you're good only because you're paid to be good, when the money runs out, so will your integrity.

Are you more concerned with receiving a paycheck than doing your job with excellence? Do you fulfill your commitments to yourself and others? When faced with the temptation to do wrong, do you choose the right path? Integrity is a part of good character—if people can't count on you to do what you say you'll do, you won't be taken seriously.

Identify one person you know who has maintained integrity during times when it would have been easier for him or her to make a different choice. What can you do to emulate that behavior? What steps can you take in your personal life to build your integrity? Before you can improve integrity where other people are concerned, you must build it in yourself, so set a standard for yourself in every area, from finances to relationships, and stick to it. You'll feel better about yourself and build your character when you commit to live a life of integrity.

Daily Quotes

"Always do right. This will gratify some people, and astonish the rest."

— Mark Twain

"The ultimate measure of a man is not where he stands in moments of comfort and convenience, but where he stands at times of challenge and controversy."

— Dr. Martin Luther King, Jr.

"Integrity without knowledge is weak and useless, and knowledge without integrity is dangerous and dreadful."

— Samuel Johnson

lo
VE

love Intense affection for another
arising out of kinship or personal ties.
A feeling that produces unconditional
commitment and loyalty to another.

Day 21

Love:
Share It

Definition of *love:*
Intense affection for another
arising out of kinship or personal
ties. A feeling that produces
unconditional commitment
and loyalty to another.

Say It

As you speak the following phrases, believe and
embrace them. Visualize yourself having what you
state—possess it. Notice how your voice and body
respond to each "I" statement:

- *I acknowledge the importance of
  unconditional love.*

- *I possess an attitude of unconditional love.*

- *I am in love with life.*

- *I am in love with the things of God.*

- *I am a person of unparalleled love.*

Believe It

Love should be the foundation from which everything else in your life is built. Take, for example, Derek Redmond, a British runner in the 400-meter race at the 1992 Olympics. Derek was leading at the first turn when a sharp pain in the back of his right thigh threw him to the track in agony with a torn hamstring muscle. Pure determination and desire caused Derek to get up and continue the race with no hope of winning a medal. But the tenacity alone of this dedicated runner couldn't get him to the finish line. His father, Jim, left his seat in the stands, pushed aside the security guards, and made his way to his son on the track. Arm in arm, shoulder to shoulder, father and son got to the finish line, which Jim allowed Derek to cross on his own. Derek Redmond finished the race to a standing ovation, and even though he didn't win a medal that day, he and his father taught the world about the power of love.

Love, when shared, makes us *all* winners, because it's concerned with giving and not taking. Love is the nature of God, and when you become more concerned with helping others achieve their goals, you find that things begin to work out for you, too. Making a decision to walk in love will propel you to a life of never-ending achievement.

Receive It

Think of someone who needs your love, and call, e-mail, fax, or write him or her today. In your quiet time, imagine your love bubbling up from the very bottom of your spine. Feel it rise up through your hips, to your stomach, across your chest, all around your heart, and into your head. Feel it inside you . . . and imagine how much you have to give. The next time you have the opportunity to give away a little love, remember how filled you are with it. You can never run out of love, for you manufacture it every day. Give affection to others freely and without expectation, just as the earth gives us its foundation to stand upon without expecting anything in return.

Many people who have had near-death experiences return to the living and reveal the great message they received as they almost made a transition to the other side: "The message is love—we must love one another."

Of course you don't need to come close to death to learn to live your life in love. Let it drive all your actions: Love your enemies, love your friends, and love yourself. The more love you give away, the more it comes back to you, multiplied.

Daily Quotes

"Let God love you through others and let God love others through you."

— D. M. Street

"Never forget that the most powerful force on earth is love."

— Nelson Rockefeller

"Three of the strongest words in the world to motivate anyone happen to be the three least used: 'I love you.' And four of the strongest are: 'I love you, too.'"

— Keith D. Harrell

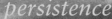

persistence
Continuing firmly and steadfastly
despite obstacles; to continue
in existence: enduring.

perSIST
ence

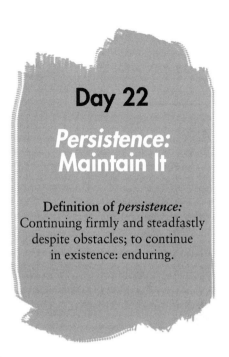

Day 22

Persistence: Maintain It

Definition of *persistence*:
Continuing firmly and steadfastly
despite obstacles; to continue
in existence: enduring.

Say It

As you speak the following phrases, believe and
embrace them. Visualize yourself having what you
state—possess it. Notice how your voice and body
respond to each "I" statement:

- *I acknowledge the importance of being persistent.*

- *I keep going until I reach my goal.*

- *I possess an inner drive of persistence.*

- *I am set up to keep going; I succeed by being persistent.*

- *I am persistent and will always press on.*

Believe It

A persistent person *always* gets what he or she wants, so never stop believing in yourself and striving to achieve your goals. Remember that nothing in the world can stop the success of a person who has dogged determination. In the game of life, persistence and purpose are power twins that remain undefeated. If you adopt these qualities in your own life, you can't help but see your goals begin to manifest.

When Harold chose to leave high school to enlist in the Navy, for instance, he dreamed that all of his children would have the opportunity to attend college. Throughout his life he often held down several jobs—sometimes working all day *and* all night—to make ends meet. Yet when times got tough, Harold never gave up. He was persistent in achieving his goals, which were providing for his family and making sure that his children had the opportunities he never had. Everything he wanted eventually came to him, because he never gave up, caved in, or quit.

Persistence is remaining focused on the task at hand, no matter what's going on around you. Harold could have easily thrown in the towel from the stress and pressure he was facing, but it was his ability to look adversity in the face that helped him continue to press toward the mark and ultimately succeed in life.

Receive It

How would you rate your persistence—do you have an unstoppable attitude? Quietly meditate on the events in your life that thwarted you: Were they outside challenges, or did issues within yourself slow you down? What could you have done to get around those barriers and move on toward your goal? How will you handle the next obstacle that you perceive in your life? Will you sit down and give up, or will you find a way over, under, around, or through whatever gets in your way? Now that you know that persistence is key to reaching your goals, I hope you understand that if you keep plugging away at whatever gets in your way, it *will* give way.

Life just can't beat the person who keeps coming back, the person who never, ever gives up. Most of the time, when you remain steadfast in the face of challenges, you acquire the strength necessary to see things through to the end. You see, persistence will build up your ability to endure. You won't get intimidated by negativity, but instead will feel a sense of empowerment in knowing that you didn't let anything deter you. The difference between those who quit and those who press on is simply a spirit of persistence. It's a decision. In every champion, you'll find one key ingredient: an attitude of unshakable determination.

Daily Quotes

"I have learned that success is to be measured not so much by the position that one has reached in life as by the obstacles which he has overcome while trying to succeed."

— Booker T. Washington

"Nothing in the world can take the place of a person who is persistent. In the game of life, persistence remains undefeated."

— Bruce Harrell

"When someone tells you to keep going, that's encouraging. When you tell yourself, 'Don't stop,' that's powerful, but when God says, 'Persist until you win,' your victory then becomes guaranteed."

— Keith D. Harrell

෨෨   ෨෨   ෨෨

Possi BILity

possibility
Capable of existing or being true; capable of happening or being accomplished; potential; capable of being used for a certain purpose.

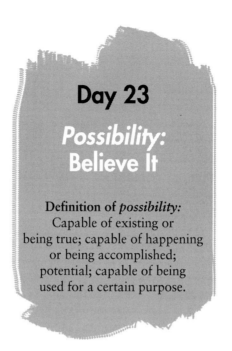

Day 23

Possibility:
Believe It

Definition of *possibility*:
Capable of existing or
being true; capable of happening
or being accomplished;
potential; capable of being
used for a certain purpose.

Say It

As you speak the following phrases, believe and
embrace them. Visualize yourself having what you
state—possess it. Notice how your voice and body
respond to each "I" statement:

- *I acknowledge that there are unlimited
  possibilities for my life.*

- *I possess the awareness that possibility
  encompasses my life.*

- *I am aware that with God, all things are possible.*

- *I am always thinking about the possibilities.*

- *I am not swayed by what things look like on the outside. Anything is possible.*

Believe It

Have confidence that endless possibilities for your life can happen at any moment. For example, I realized this when I won the National Speakers Association (NSA) Council of Peers Award for Excellence in 2000, which put me in the NSA Hall of Fame. I was overwhelmed by emotion when I received this recognition, since being recognized by my peers as one of the top speakers in the country was a great honor. Who would have ever thought that this tall, shy, skinny kid who stuttered for most of his childhood would one day be inducted into the NSA Hall of Fame? God knew that there was a possibility, and He made it happen because through Him, all things are possible.

A similar story has to do with a man named Sanford, who decided to go to veterinary school. He was three years older than most of the other students because he'd taken time after receiving his undergraduate degree to work in a lab at the Johns Hopkins University School of Medicine. Others who had tried to get into veterinary school told him it was impossible—each school had only a few spaces available, and truly determined students would win those spots. Most of those students had dedicated their lives to becoming veterinarians, while Sanford had thought he wanted to go into medical school before he changed his mind.

Sanford refused to listen to the naysayers who told him not to even try, and he applied to the only veterinary school in his area, hoping to win one of the few seats available. As part of the entry, he had to write an essay explaining why he wanted to be a veterinarian. He poignantly described the fact that as an only child, animals were his only siblings—and the essay earned him an alternate spot. Someone must have withdrawn his or her application, because Sanford soon received notice he could enter veterinary college immediately. Even though other people frowned on the idea of Sanford achieving his dream, he knew he could make it happen.

Receive It

Consider the things you would do if you knew that absolutely anything was possible. Would you learn to fly an airplane? Take a different course with your career? Travel around the world? You can do all these things and more, for you have the potential to do, be, or have whatever you set your mind to. Start by believing in the probability of the occurrence, and in time, your dream will become your reality. God will make sure of it. If you can imagine it, the possibilities are limitless—all you have to do is give yourself permission to accomplish it.

Daily Quotes

"We are all given possibilities to do and be whatever we want."

— Anonymous

"Look at things as they can be, not as they are, and you'll gradually see the possibilities."

— Keith D. Harrell

". . . with God, all things are possible."

— Matthew 19:26

ʘ ʘ ʘ

purpose

Desire, goal, aim, intention.
The object toward which
one strives or for which
something exists.

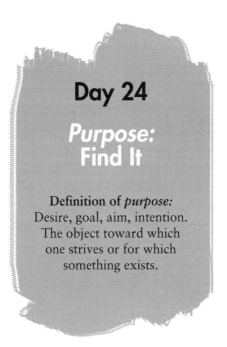

Day 24

Purpose:
Find It

Definition of *purpose:*
Desire, goal, aim, intention.
The object toward which
one strives or for which
something exists.

Say It

As you speak the following phrases, believe and embrace them. Visualize yourself having what you state—possess it. Notice how your voice and body respond to each "I" statement:

- *I acknowledge my purpose.*

- *I possess a purpose for my life.*

- *I am living each day with purpose and passion.*

- *I am fulfilling God's purpose for my life.*

- *I am willing to stretch and grow in order to fulfill my appointed purpose.*

Believe It

Before I discovered my purpose in life, my work wasn't fulfilling. I felt a void inside until I finally discovered that I was put on this planet to make a positive mark in the lives of others by getting them to understand the power of their attitude. Today, I show others the role that their attitude plays in their lives, and my mission is to make people fully understand and embrace the philosophy that "attitude is everything."

Now that I know my mission, I can make sure that everything I do brings me closer to my goal. Knowing my purpose helps me make life-changing decisions easily. Having a clear vision of why I'm here keeps me aligned and on target for my goals. (And whenever I need instructions for my life, I just read the Bible, which stands for Basic Instructions Before Leaving Earth.)

Receive It

If you've been unable to reach your goals, perhaps it's because they weren't in alignment with your true purpose. You need to ask yourself what your reason for living is. If you haven't found what lights your fire yet, you must do so before you can define your goals. So take some quiet time to meditate on your purpose in life. Go inside to figure out what you want to do, for whom, and why you want to do it. When you find your answers, write them down and keep refining and defining them until you have a one-sentence statement that outlines your mission in life. Once you have that one-sentence "purpose statement" down, you'll be on your way to achieving whatever it is you truly want from life.

There are two great moments in a person's life: The first is when you're born; the second is when you discover *why* you were born. Purpose is like the drum major leading the band—it's out front directing the way, in step with harmony and rhythm.

Daily Quotes

"Purpose is what gives life a meaning."
— C. H. Parkhurst

*"The world stands aside to let anyone pass
who knows where he is going."*
— David Starr Jordan

*"I think the purpose of life is to be useful,
to be responsible, to be honorable, to be
compassionate. It is, above all, to matter: to
count, to stand for something, to have made
some difference that you lived at all."*
— Leo C. Rosten

risK

risk
The possibility of
suffering harm
or loss; danger.

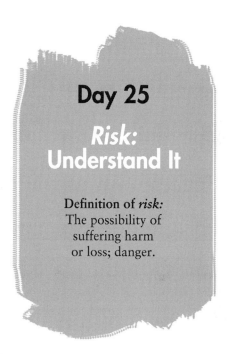

Day 25

Risk: Understand It

Definition of *risk*:
The possibility of
suffering harm
or loss; danger.

Say It

As you speak the following phrases, believe and
embrace them. Visualize yourself having what you
state—possess it. Notice how your voice and body
respond to each "I" statement:

- *I acknowledge the importance of
  taking risks.*

- *I possess the ability to take risks.*

- *I step toward all risks with the attitude, faith, and power to conquer.*

- *I am a risk taker. I take risks knowing that sound thinking produces exceptional results.*

- *I am willing to take the necessary risks to succeed.*

Believe It

Going to work for myself has been one of the biggest risks I've ever taken. I'd worked for IBM for 14 years, and it was my first and only job. Yet I knew that I wanted to help others succeed, and to do that, I had to take some chances and make changes in my life. I risked my money, my time, and my future, knowing that if I didn't, I'd never move toward my ultimate goal. Taking the gamble was well worth it, as my career as a motivational speaker has turned out even better than I ever fantasized it would. Going after my dream enabled me to meet new people and make a difference in the lives of hundreds of thousands of people. At the same time, while I have impacted their lives, many of these people have greatly affected *me* as well.

Looking back on it, my risks seem really small in comparison to the giant rewards I've reaped as a result of taking those leaps of faith.

Receive It

In the game of life, some people show up to watch, some to cheer, and some to play. To get in the game, you've got to take some risks. Doing something you've never done before means that you're going to have to move out of your comfort zone. For example, you may have to leave your family and friends, nice house, or well-paying job—and even though it may seem difficult at first, you must overcome your fears so that you'll get on that road to success.

Take time to consider the chances you must take if you wish to attain your long-term goals. Write them down and look at the pros and cons. Study the odds, but expect the unexpected. And keep in mind that being successful means that you risk being a failure—but if you're paralyzed with fear, you'll never give yourself the chance to make it at all.

To deal with risk and reach your full potential, you must develop a "whatever it takes" attitude. Reduce your gamble by following the three *P*'s: preparation, planning, and prayer. If you seek God's direction, your roll of the dice will turn into a stepping-stone to success. Remember, when you take a chance, the only downside is failure. Yet sometimes failure merely keeps you in the same place, so you've risked nothing at all. Measure your odds, recheck your backup plan, and go for it! You'll never know what could have happened if you don't take that first step.

Daily Quotes

*"Take calculated risks. That is quite
different from being rash."*

— General George S. Patton, Jr.

*"Living at risk is jumping off the cliff and
building your wings on the way down."*

— Ray Bradbury

*"And the trouble is, if you don't risk anything,
you risk even more."*

— Erica Jong

sacri
FICE

sacrifice
Forfeiture of
something
valuable for the sake
of something else.

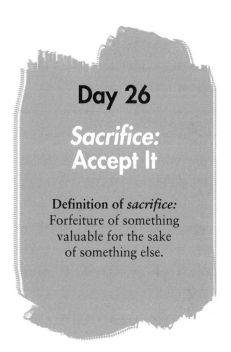

Day 26

Sacrifice:
Accept It

Definition of *sacrifice:*
Forfeiture of something
valuable for the sake
of something else.

Say It

As you speak the following phrases, believe and
embrace them. Visualize yourself having what you
state—possess it. Notice how your voice and body
respond to each "I" statement:

- *I acknowledge the things I need to
  sacrifice.*

- *I possess the ability to sacrifice in
  order to succeed.*

- *I am making a sacrifice for my family, whom I love very much.*

- *I am able to make sacrifices.*

- *I am willing to sacrifice now so that my family and I can benefit later.*

Believe It

Sacrifice is one of the hardest things you'll have to do on the road to success, but to get what you want out of life, you're going to have to give something up. For example, if you want to live a more rewarding spiritual life, one that pleases God, you'll have to give up the things that will lead you down the wrong path.

Sacrifice is inevitable—when I think of this concept, I think of my grandparents and parents, who forfeited personal time to raise a family. I think of the people in the armed forces, who risk their lives to protect this country. I think of teachers, who give up the chance at higher-paying careers to help all of us. I think of all the volunteers in the world, including men and women in the ministry, who donate their time to serve others and/or build them up spiritually. All of these people have made the world a better place.

Personally, I've given up the chance to have a family so that I could more easily pursue my business goals and aspirations. I had to do this to see my dreams come to pass. As I get older and reflect on my life, I sure hope that I'll be able to say that the sacrifice was worth it, but I don't know. I simply have to trust that the opportunities I gave up weren't as important or wouldn't have had as positive an impact as the things I chose to do.

Receive It

In life, you must make a commitment, take action, and come to realize that sacrifice is also part of the package. Everything you desire to achieve comes with a catch, or something you must give up to reach your dream. Are you willing to pay that price? If not, perhaps your goal isn't really worth it. As you examine what you must give up in order to get what you want out of life, you'll recognize the opportunity to evaluate how badly you want to reach your desired destination. If it isn't worth the time, effort, or end result, give it up! However, if your dream *is* worth giving something up, then the sacrifices you make to reach it will seem small in comparison.

Spend some time thinking about your goals and what you're willing to give up to reach them—for only you can decide what you're willing to give up or do without in order to win.

Daily Quotes

"If you want to achieve little, sacrifice little."

— Anonymous

"I stand here before you not as a prophet but as a humble servant of you, the people. Your tireless and heroic sacrifices have made it possible for me to be here today. I therefore place the remaining years of my life in your hands."

— Nelson Mandela

"By sacrificing, you're choosing to do your best in order to have what you truly desire."

— Anonymous

self-esteem
Having a
high regard,
or respect
for oneself.

self-
ESTEEM

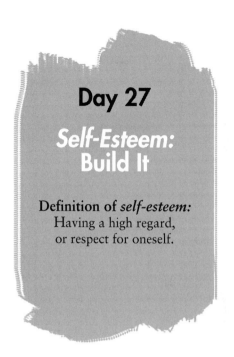

Day 27

Self-Esteem: Build It

Definition of *self-esteem:*
Having a high regard,
or respect for oneself.

Say It

As you speak the following phrases, believe
and embrace them. Visualize yourself having what
you state—possess it. Notice how your voice and
body respond to each "I" statement:

- *I acknowledge the importance of having high self-esteem.*

- *I possess high self-esteem.*

- *I am my own unconditional best friend.*

- *I am one of God's precious gifts.*

- *I am a winner.*

Believe It

Everyone experiences self-doubt or dissatisfaction at different times. One period in my life particularly stands out. During my freshman year in college, my basketball team had a poor season, winning only 5 games and losing 17—a personal worst for me. Up to that point, I'd never looked at myself as a loser, but my confidence started to wane dramatically during this time. I doubted my skills and my ability to play well, and I became so depressed that I questioned whether life was even worth living. My whole identity was tied up in basketball.

The summer after that horrible freshman year, I decided to turn things around by practicing, working hard on the fundamentals of the game, and looking ahead to the upcoming season. As a result, I pulled myself out of my slump. I realized that I couldn't do anything about the past, but I could make a difference in the future. By taking the necessary steps to improve my game, I was able to rebuild my self-esteem. It was just a matter of doing my part to boost myself back up—and realizing that nobody else could do it for me.

Receive It

Don't confuse self-esteem with arrogance: Arrogance is an overevaluation of your worth, while self-esteem is a healthy opinion of yourself—it's valuing yourself to the point that you don't allow other people or negative situations and circumstance to influence the way you feel about yourself. Until you value yourself, you won't value anything, and other people won't value you either. After all, your relationship with yourself is the most important one you'll ever have.

When you're filled with self-doubt, give yourself a little pep talk. Repeat aloud the following, "A 30-Second Commercial to Me":

> "[YOUR NAME], you are great! You are a unique individual, a new kind of person the world has never known. You were born to do well. You were born to succeed. You were born to bless the lives of others. You were born to be great, and you have what it

takes to be great. You are enthusiastic, optimistic, and a change-embracer. You are a giver rather than a taker. You are organized. You are a hard worker. You are happy. You are a master over yourself; you are a leader. You are a big thinker. As blessed as you are with all these talents, there isn't one thing in the world you can't do. You will never fail. [YOUR NAME], go out and make today an 'attitude is everything' day!"

By making this profession every day, you'll experience an awesome self-esteem boost! Remember, you are priceless—your past is history, and your future is now.

Daily Quotes

*"No one can make you feel inferior
without your consent."*

— Eleanor Roosevelt

*"Until you value yourself,
you won't value anything."*

— Anonymous

*"If you make friends with yourself,
you will never be alone."*

— Maxwell Maltz

SETback

setback

An unanticipated delay
or reverse in progress.

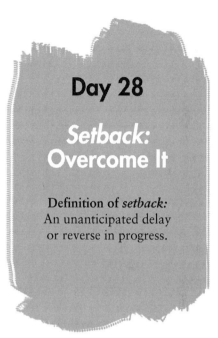

Day 28

Setback: Overcome It

Definition of *setback:*
An unanticipated delay
or reverse in progress.

Say It

As you speak the following phrases, believe and embrace them. Visualize yourself having what you state—possess it. Notice how your voice and body respond to each "I" statement:

- *I acknowledge that there will be setbacks.*

- *I possess the ability to overcome setbacks.*

- *I am able to handle adversity because I know it will pass.*

- *I am learning valuable lessons from each setback.*

- *I am strong, turning my setbacks into comebacks.*

Believe It

Setbacks are only turning points waiting to be converted into learning points. I've definitely had experience with life's stumbling blocks, and in my early days at IBM, I experienced an especially disheartening one. I watched someone on my sales team make the 100% Club (a prestigious honor at the company), while I was overlooked for no apparent reason. Both of us received training together and worked as a team with the same customers, so I simply couldn't understand why I'd been passed over. Yet instead of dwelling on the situation, I looked at what I could learn from it and then decided to put myself in charge of my destiny. With the help of my new manager, Craig Karis, the following year I made it into the 100% Club. That experience taught me that when life knocks you down, it doesn't knock you out unless you let it. I also learned not to trust other people for my promotions—advancement comes from God and, in due season, it will come to pass.

You may have experienced similar disappointments. Just know that the key to coming out on top of such situations is to recognize that setbacks are just a part of life. Things aren't always going to go according to your plans and timing, but have faith that if you do your part, in God's time you're going to experience the success that you expect and believe will come.

Receive It

Don't dwell on failures—instead, learn what you can from them and continue to move toward your goal. For every win and loss, there's a lesson to be learned. Usually setbacks will reveal something about yourself that you didn't even know, such as a poor attitude or impatience. After all, without life's ups and downs, you'd never discover your own strengths.

Do you feel as if you've had too many setbacks? If so, examine them. Life always serves you a lesson—if you don't learn it, you'll get served that same lesson again and again. So learn from your setback!

Write down three things that you've accomplished or three things that have had significant meaning in your life, and think about what you did to achieve them. How did you overcome the delays and disappointment along the way? If you had nothing holding you back from your goal, achieving it wouldn't have had any merit. The setbacks made you stronger—so welcome them, learn from them, and get over them. And remember that a setback is nothing but a setup for something better.

Daily Quotes

"Anything other than death is a minor injury."

— Bill Muncey

*"Turn your setback into
a set up for something better."*

— Willie Jolley

*"For every win and loss, there is a lesson in
disguise. Without life's joys and defeats, you would
never know the stock of which you are made."*

— Keith D. Harrell

success The achievement of
something desired, intended or attempted.

sucCESS

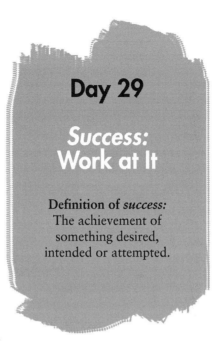

Day 29

Success:
Work at It

Definition of *success*:
The achievement of
something desired,
intended or attempted.

Say It

As you speak the following phrases, believe and
embrace them. Visualize yourself having what you
state—possess it. Notice how your voice and body
respond to each "I" statement:

- *I acknowledge that I have the skills
  needed for success.*

- *I possess the skills needed for success
  in all areas of my life.*

- *I am a winner. Success follows me wherever I go.*

- *I am drawn to success. I act as if I have already succeeded.*

- *I am empowered to succeed, and I encourage others to be successful.*

Believe It

There is a seed of greatness inside you that has the potential to grow and produce success in every area of your life, from your finances to your relationships. God created you with winning in mind—whether or not you recognize this will determine how far you go. You must come to understand and believe that no matter how big or how small, success at *any* level is meaningful. So cultivate your desire for winning by seeing yourself accomplishing your goals with ease.

Remind yourself right now that you're accomplishing something each day you wake up. Every day you're being propelled to the next level. Your success doesn't depend on your race, age, gender, or occupation—what matters is your attitude and mind-set. If you believe that you can succeed, you will.

It's important to achieve in life because success builds your self-esteem and empowers you to take on more challenges and have a positive outcome. However, it's essential that you judge your accomplishments by your own standards and not someone else's. Success may mean something different to you than it does for someone else: One person may think it means becoming a millionaire, while another may find it in having a family. Whatever your idea of success is, pursue it with all you've got so that you can see it materialize in your life.

My friend Alicia told me about having to take a class in home economics when she was in junior high school. To pass the class, she had to sew a blouse . . . only she didn't know the first thing about sewing, so she feared that she'd fail in her attempts. Her mother gave her money to buy the material and sent her on her way—yet Alicia had no idea where to buy fabric, and she didn't even know how much she needed. She felt lost in the huge five-and-dime: The scared 12-year-old wandered down aisle after aisle until she came upon a package filled with hideous pink cloth. She had enough money to buy it, so she did (along with matching thread). When she got home, her mother laughed at what she'd purchased. "You have ten times what you need for a blouse," she said, "and just look at that color! It doesn't go with anything!"

Alicia felt defeated, but she decided that if she finished the blouse, it didn't matter if she ever wore it—she would have accomplished something significant. She took the package to class, and the teacher showed all the students the necessary techniques to sew their own blouses. All the other girls had selected stylish plaids and appealing solid colors. Hers was the only outrageously pink bolt of fabric in the room. No matter—weeks later, Alicia put the last stitches into the hem of her sickly pink blouse. It had a few flaws, and she never wore it, but she passed the course, and subsequently realized that she could do anything she set her mind to do. Alicia had succeeded in the way *she* defined success.

Receive It

To win, you have to work hard, play by the rules, and most important, stay in the game. You can't allow situations, circumstances, and other people's opinions of you to affect whether or not you're going to succeed in life—these things should be viewed simply as obstacles to overcome.

Reflect on one of your successes. How did you feel when you accomplished what you'd set for yourself? Write down how you accomplished this goal in a detailed manner so that you have a blueprint to work with. Now take action! Finally, don't confuse success with wealth, popularity, or fame. Success is personal, and everyone's definition of it is different, so celebrate every positive step you take, no matter how small.

Daily Quotes

*"The best place to succeed is where
you are with what you have."*

— Charles M. Schwab

*"If your success is not on your terms,
if it looks good to the world but does not feel
good in your heart, it is not success at all."*

— Anna Quindlen

*"Creating success is tough, but keeping it is
tougher. You have to keep producing,
you can never stop."*

— Pete Rose

wisdom
Insightful
understanding
of what
is right,
true, or
enduring;
good
judgment;
knowledge;
discretion;
skill in the
management
of affairs.

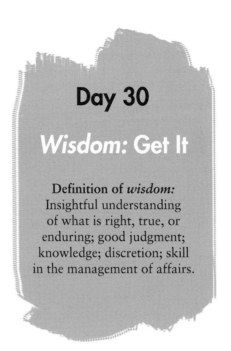

Day 30

Wisdom: Get It

Definition of *wisdom:*
Insightful understanding
of what is right, true, or
enduring; good judgment;
knowledge; discretion; skill
in the management of affairs.

Say It

As you speak the following phrases, believe and
embrace them. Visualize yourself having what you
state—possess it. Notice how your voice and body
respond to each "I" statement:

- *I acknowledge wisdom as the
  principal thing.*

- *I possess wisdom in all that I do.*

- *I am using wisdom to do all things.*

- *I am filled with the wisdom of God.*

- *I am wiser today than I was yesterday because of the wisdom instilled in me.*

Believe It

I learned from my spiritual parents, Dr. Creflo Dollar and Taffi Dollar of World Changers Church International, that wisdom is the ability to use what you know. It's much more than just having a lot of information or "head knowledge"—it's knowing what to do when you aren't sure what logical path to take. For example, many people have been to college and have acquired extensive degrees in their fields, but when they're in a "crunch," they're at a loss as to how to solve their problems and challenges. They need wisdom, which is the key to unlocking the answers to life's problems.

Our church motto is: "Wisdom is the principal thing; therefore get wisdom: and with all thy getting, get understanding" (Proverbs 4:7). This is a powerful statement because until you really understand something, you can't put it to use.

Therefore, wisdom must be a fundamental part of your life, for it's an invaluable key to success.

Receive It

Many times you take steps and make decisions without being backed by wisdom. Often, when this happens, the choices you make aren't the best ones, and you end up wasting time and energy. It's critical that you seek God's wisdom first in all your decisions. When you're angry, tired, or emotional, you're less likely to have sound judgment, so don't make any moves without spending some time alone to hear from God. During these quiet moments, think of any area where you may need more information or understanding about a particular situation. Listen for an inner knowing or voice that will guide and direct you as to how to proceed.

In relationships, problems sometimes arise when you don't understand your partner's needs and goals. Once you truly understand the other person, there's no need to argue. The same is true with any other challenging situation—what you don't understand will create conflict, which is why understanding and wisdom are critical to your success.

The phrase "knowledge is power" is true; however, a more correct statement would be "knowledge combined with wisdom is power." The two go hand in hand, for you need wisdom to put the knowledge you have to good use. Wisdom can be looked at as the spark that ignites the flame of knowledge. Gaining more information is the first step—if you're having trouble reaching a goal, think about what you may not yet have learned. Do you need to learn how to write better so you can sell your short stories and novels? Do you need to understand politics better so you can win an election? Ponder the areas where your information base could increase, and then find the resources you need. Once you have the information, ask God how to use that information as a stepping-stone to success and the achievement of your goals . . . that's wisdom.

Daily Quotes

*"Wisdom never kicks at the iron
walls it can't bring down."*

— Oliver Schreiner

*"Wisdom is a key element for
succeeding in life."*

— Anonymous

*"To acquire knowledge, one must study;
but to acquire wisdom, one must observe."*

— Marilyn vos Savant

It's now time to challenge life by realizing how
the 30 key words we've examined can help
change your attitude and ultimately help change
your life. Remember, attitude is everything,
so say it, believe it, and receive it!

ACKNOWLEDGMENTS

I was blessed to have the help and support of many talented people to whom I want to express my sincere thanks:

To my wonderful staff, Donna Cash and Deborah Johnson, for all their help and support.

To Jill Kramer and Shannon Littrell, my editors, for their insight and expertise; as well as designer Amy Rose Szalkiewicz and all of the wonderful staff at Hay House.

To my literary agents, Jan Miller and Shannon Mizer-Marven, for their help and support.

To my sister, Toni Malliet, for her guidance and support. When I need her, she always comes through.

To Wanda Williams, for her dedication, help, and support.

Special thanks to my friend Arabella Grayson for her countless hours of insight and enduring support.

And finally, to the many individuals who have in their own special way contributed to the creation of this book: Sam Horn, Doug Smart, Suzanne Mohr, Bobbie Christmas, T.J. Roach, and Lisa Daniels.

ABOUT THE AUTHOR

Known across corporate America for his energetic, innovative presentations, **Keith D. Harrell** is a dynamic life coach and motivational speaker. Harrell shares his powerful message, "Attitude Is Everything" with audiences around the world. While growing up in Seattle, Washington, he aspired to become a professional basketball player. Although he never realized that dream, an article in *The Wall Street Journal* referred to him as a "Star with Attitude. . . . What sets him apart from less successful speakers is driving ambition, and an attitude that refuses to flag."

As president of Harrell Performance Systems, Harrell has created a firm specializing in helping those in the corporate marketplace achieve and maintain their goals through the power of a positive attitude. He is a certified speaker, trainer, and consultant and has addressed many of America's top corporations, including AT&T, Microsoft, and Kodak. Harrell counts "Big Blue" (IBM) and several other companies such as Coca-Cola among his repeat clients. His signature keynote address focuses on ways to meet the challenges of changing technology by understanding the power of human technology.

Harrell earned his bachelor's degree in community service from Seattle University before embarking on a 14-year career with IBM, where he was recognized as one of its top sales and training instructors. In 1997, he received Certified Speaking Professional designation from the National Speakers Association. In 2000, Harrell was inducted into the NSA Speaker Hall of Fame, a lifetime award for speaking excellence and professionalism. And one of the country's leading lecture agencies has put him on its list of "22 Guaranteed Standing Ovations."

෨

Please let Keith know how this book has helped you. Write to him at Harrell Performance Systems, Inc., P.O. Box 81268, Atlanta GA 30366; or visit his Website at: **www.keithharrell.com.**

HAY HOUSE TITLES OF RELATED INTEREST

BOOKS

A Deep Breath of Life, by Alan Cohen

I Can Do It®, by Louise L. Hay (book with CD)

Inner Peace for Busy People,
by Joan Z. Borysenko, Ph.D.

Life's Lessons and Reflections, by Montel Williams

Life's a Journey—Not a Sprint,
by Jennifer Lewis-Hall

Simple Things,
by Jim Brickman, with Cindy Pearlman

10 Secrets for Success and Inner Peace,
by Dr. Wayne W. Dyer

CARD DECKS

Comfort Cards, by Max Lucado

Empowerment Cards, by Tavis Smiley

If Life Is a Game, These Are the Rules Cards,
by Chérie Carter-Scott, Ph.D.

The Prayer of Jabez™ Cards
and *The Secret of the Vine™ Cards*,
by Dr. Bruce Wilkinson

The 7 Habits of Highly Effective People,
by Stephen R. Covey

All of the above are available at your local
bookstore, or may be ordered by visiting:
Hay House USA: **www.hayhouse.com**
Hay House Australia: **www.hayhouse.com.au**
Hay House UK: **www.hayhouse.co.uk**
Hay House South Africa: **orders@psdprom.co.za**

❧ NOTES ❧

❧ NOTES ❧

ༀ NOTES ༀ

⊚ NOTES ⊚

NOTES

∾ NOTES ∾

൭ **NOTES** ൭

Sign up via the Hay House USA Website to receive the Hay House online newsletter and stay informed about what's going on with your favorite authors. You'll receive bimonthly announcements about: Discounts and Offers, Special Events, Product Highlights, Free Excerpts, Giveaways, and more!

We hope you enjoyed this Hay House book. If you would like
to receive a free catalog featuring additional Hay House
books and products, or if you would like information about
the Hay Foundation, please contact:

Hay House, Inc., P.O. Box 5100
Carlsbad, CA 92018-5100

(760) 431-7695 or **(800) 654-5126**
(760) 431-6948 (fax) or **(800) 650-5115 (fax)**
www.hayhouse.com

Published and distributed in Australia by:
Hay House Australia, Ltd. • 18/36 Ralph St.
Alexandria NSW 2015 • *Phone:* 612-9669-4299
Fax: 612-9669-4144 • www.hayhouse.com.au

Published and distributed in the United Kingdom by: Hay
House UK, Ltd. • Unit 202, Canalot Studios
222 Kensal Rd., London W10 5BN
Phone: 44-20-8962-1230 • *Fax:* 44-20-8962-1239
www.hayhouse.co.uk

Published and distributed in the Republic of South Africa by:
Hay House SA (Pty), Ltd., P.O. Box 990,
Witkoppen 2068 • *Phone/Fax:* 2711-7012233
orders@psdprom.co.za

Distributed in Canada by:
Raincoast • 9050 Shaughnessy St., Vancouver, B.C.
V6P 6E5 • *Phone:* (604) 323-7100 • *Fax:* (604) 323-2600